A Brief Theory
of Spycraft

A Brief Theory of Spycraft

Weaving the Tangled Web

Christopher David Costanzo

To order additional copies of this book, contact:
Xlibris
1-888-795-4274
www.Xlibris.com
Orders@Xlibris.com
808916

To all those

who may have wondered

how spies think

THE UTTERLY CONFUSING TANGLED WEB OF DECEPTION

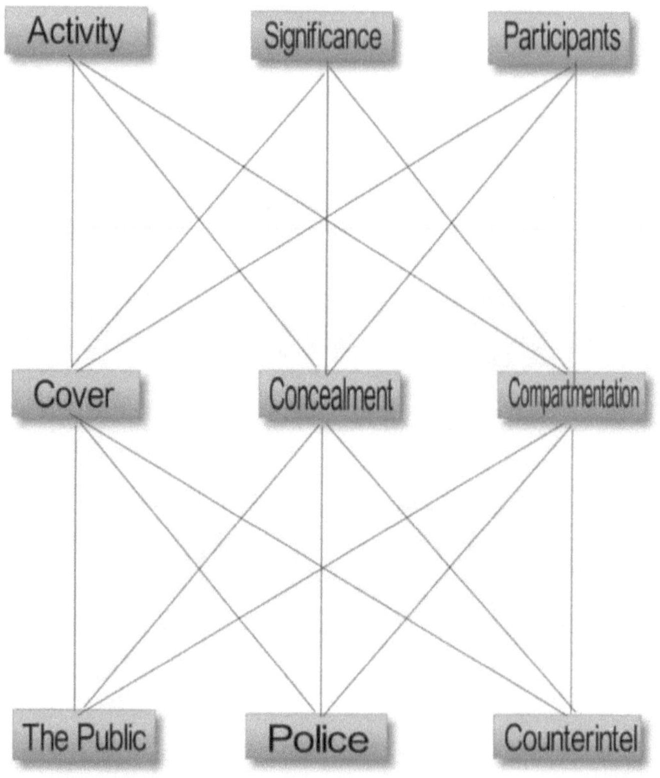

"Oh ! What a tangled web we weave when first we practice to deceive"

Sir Walter Scott

CONTENTS

INTRODUCTION

Clandestine operators do all sorts of things.

They work under cover. They work under aliases. They wear disguises. They pose as nationals of other nations. They sneak across international borders. They smuggle items into foreign countries. They operate in hostile areas where they take their lives in their hands. They recruit and manage spies. They acquire sensitive information, and they covertly manipulate the course of events abroad in support of the interests of their respective countries.

Much of their work entails serious risk. But they have at their disposal a body of principles and methods that has evolved over many centuries which enables them to protect themselves and to control the tangled web of deception that is the stock-in-trade of all clandestine operators.

This book outlines that body of principles and methods. Clandestine operators often refer to them collectively as "clandestine tradecraft," or simply as "spycraft." It was Sir Walter Scott who wrote, "Oh! What a tangled web we weave when first we practice to deceive." His observation is accurate. For that reason, good spycraft is necessary to maintain control over that inevitable tangled web inherent in clandestine operations to render them safe, productive, and worthwhile.

It requires professional clandestine operators to adopt certain patterns of thought and apply much attention to detail in order to be effective. It is a complex topic and is not for the casual reader. But if you study the principles and methods described herein, it will provide a valuable insight to the world of clandestine operations.

You will not find momentous revelations in this book. It is intended for those interested in the theory and procedures of clandestine operations beyond what one finds in most popular literature. It outlines the deeper fundamentals pertaining to one of humanity's oldest and sleaziest professions.

Did I say "sleaziest?" Indeed, I did. Throughout history, people have looked upon clandestine activity, be it human or technical, as ignoble, degenerate, and contemptible. As late as 1929, the American Secretary of State, Henry L. Stimson, shut down a secret code-breaking facility in the State Department, stating that, "Gentlemen do not read each other's mail."

Many people regard clandestine operations as particularly odious when nations carry them out with human operatives - that is, when clandestine operators persuade and manipulate people to betray their own governments and induce such people either to gather information as spies, or else to alter secretly the course of events. Nations punish such people, and the operators who manipulate them, severely and with contempt

During the American Revolution, when the Americans caught a British Major, John Andre, spying for Britain, George Washington refused to sanction Andre's execution by firing squad, which in those days was an honorable way for a soldier to die. Instead, Washington insisted on hanging Andre ignominiously. Yet, Washington himself made use of his own spies to learn the plans and intentions of British forces in America, and to scout out enemy positions.

But, as despicable as clandestine activity may seem to a well-bred lady or gentleman, nations have almost always felt compelled to engage in it. The paramount interests of a nation are its independence and security. A close secondary interest is its economic well-being. A nation may use diplomacy to protect these interests peacefully through persuasion and negotiation, or it may use war when it believes that physical coercion is necessary. But it usually finds it equally necessary to rely on espionage and covert action to support both diplomacy and war.

The immediate goal of espionage is to acquire information that is not available openly and legally. It is the pursuit of information that is not available publicly and would be useful to a nation's diplomats, to its warriors, and to those who administer its economic interests. Of course, the goal is to do it without letting others know it. So, espionage is necessarily a clandestine activity. Obviously the same is true for covert action by which a nation attempts clandestinely to influence and even manipulate the course of action of another nation.

Many people see diplomacy as a dignified profession because it relies on peaceful methods. And they regard war as a noble profession because of the great sacrifices of those who engage in it. On the other hand, they regard clandestine activity as sordid, base, and unscrupulous, whether it supports peace or war, because its stock-in-trade is deception, subterfuge, and intrigue. This book will explain how it all works.

(Note: Throughout this book we will use the contemporary word "clandestinity," rather than the more traditional word, "clandestineness.")

CHAPTER I

Basic Concepts and Operational Security

Some Definitions

Secret Agent: In addition to technical means such as overflight reconnaissance, long distance observation, and intercepts of communication, nations carry out espionage by means of controlled human sources. The operative word is "controlled," which goes beyond casual informants or elicitation. This book deals with controlled human sources who, as subordinate employees, do the bidding of the nation they secretly serve. We will call such controlled sources ***secret agents***, some of whom can also carry out covert activities to alter the course of events.

It is important to note that in the foregoing context, the label ***secret agent*** does <u>not</u> mean an official who wields government authority, such as a law enforcement official or an overt government investigative officer. It means people who do our bidding in places and in circumstances where we ourselves cannot go and where we ourselves cannot act.

Clandestine Operator: We will use the label ***clandestine operator*** to denote an individual who recruits and manages ***secret agents*** to acquire non-public information by clandestine means, or else to alter the course of events secretly.

Sponsor: We will use the word ***sponsor*** to denote the clandestine organization that employs ***clandestine operators*** who in turn recruit and manage ***secret agents***.

Customer: And we will use the word ***customer*** to denote the government on behalf of whom the ***sponsor*** carries out its activities through its ***clandestine operators*** and ***secret agents***. Typically, a ***customer*** would be any policy-making or policy-executing department of a government, or government personnel who analyze information, all of whom in turn might make use of a number of clandestine organizations as ***sponsors*** of clandestine activity to acquire such needed information.

Thus, the information that ***secret agents*** acquire flows upward to the ***clandestine operators*** to whom they report, and from there to their ***sponsors***, and finally to the ***customer*** in the form of analyzed information which we term "intelligence" (Figure 1). Later we will discuss the role of analysis in transforming "information" into "intelligence," which is an important distinction.

Examples

A typical arrangement in the Cold War was the Soviet government as a ***customer***, and the Soviet military intelligence service (the GRU) and the Soviet national security service (the KGB) as the ***sponsors*** of clandestine activity. The personnel whom these **sponsors** sent to carry out the clandestine activity would be **clandestine operators**. And, the individuals embedded in other countries and answerable to the **clandestine operators** would be the **secret agents**.

In Britain in the time of the first Queen Elizabeth, she and her council were the **customers** who required information to determine national policies. The **sponsor** of activities designed to acquire the information was the intelligence apparatus of Elizabeth's Secretary of State, Sir Francis Walsingham. The **clandestine operators** would have been the Englishmen whom Walsingham dispatched to various courts in Europe and to places within Britain on different pretexts to seek out **secret agents**. The **secret agents** would have been those in Europe and Britain whom the **clandestine operators** induced to reveal non-public information to them.

Another example might be the United States, where various government entities and analysts would be the **customers**. The Central Intelligence Agency's Clandestine Service would be a **sponsor**. Its personnel would be its **clandestine operators**, and their sources would be its **secret agents**.

The Importance of Acquiring and Protecting Secret Agents

Although openly-available information is certainly essential for understanding political, economic and military realities, it should be obvious that non-public information, which a government can glean only by clandestine means, can be equally important if not more so. For the foregoing reason, the acquisition of well-placed **secret agents** is the critical goal of clandestine activity.

FLOW OF INFORMATION

Figure 1

Acquiring agents, handling them, communicating with them, manipulating their activities, and conveying the information that comes from them, are the basic skills known collectively as spycraft. So is the practice of counterintelligence to ensure that, conversely, others don't have agents working against one's own activities. A body of doctrine has developed over the centuries regarding these age-old disciplines. This book will elucidate all these doctrines in a modern setting.

<u>Fundamental to the practice of all clandestine activity are the principles of operational security to protect the secrecy of all such activity</u>.

Operational Security in a Nutshell

There are really only three things to protect. Only three forces from which to protect them. And only three methods of protection:

To be protected are:

    a) ***the existence of a clandestine activity,***
    b) ***the significance of the activity, and***
    c) ***the identity of its participants.***

They must be protected from three opposing forces:

    a) ***the public,***
    b) ***law enforcers, and***
    c) ***professional counterintelligence services.***

The three methods for protecting them are:

    a) ***cover,***
    b) ***concealment, and***
    c) ***compartmentation.***

It is absolutely essential that clandestine operators and their secret agents cultivate a deep understanding of the foregoing principles. If you learn these principles thoroughly (and we will elucidate their application throughout this book), you will be well on the way towards mastering the craft of clandestinity. It will allow you to control the "tangled web" of deception rather than let it control you.

<u>The application of three methods to protect three aspects of clandestine activity from three types of opposition thereby requires an analysis of twenty-seven interactions. Hence the "tangled web" of deception, which all clandestine operators must grasp in detail.</u> (Figure 2).

Applying the Elements of Operational Security

Assume you are a clandestine operator abroad and that you meet regularly with your secret agent who works in the local Ministry of Defense. Of course, you would prefer that nobody know that someone in the Ministry of Defense is in contact with a foreigner (that is, you prefer that nobody know of the existence of the ***activity***). But if it were known, you certainly do not want anyone to know the reason why you two are meeting (that is, the ***significance*** of the contact). And, of course, if you are observed in contact with each other, you do not want anyone to know who you are, or who the person with whom you are in contact is (that is, the identities of the ***participants*** in the activity).

In addition, you must have a clear perception regarding from whom you are protecting your clandestine activities. And in this regard, there are three threats to protect against.

OPERATIONAL SECURITY
Thinking Like a Professional

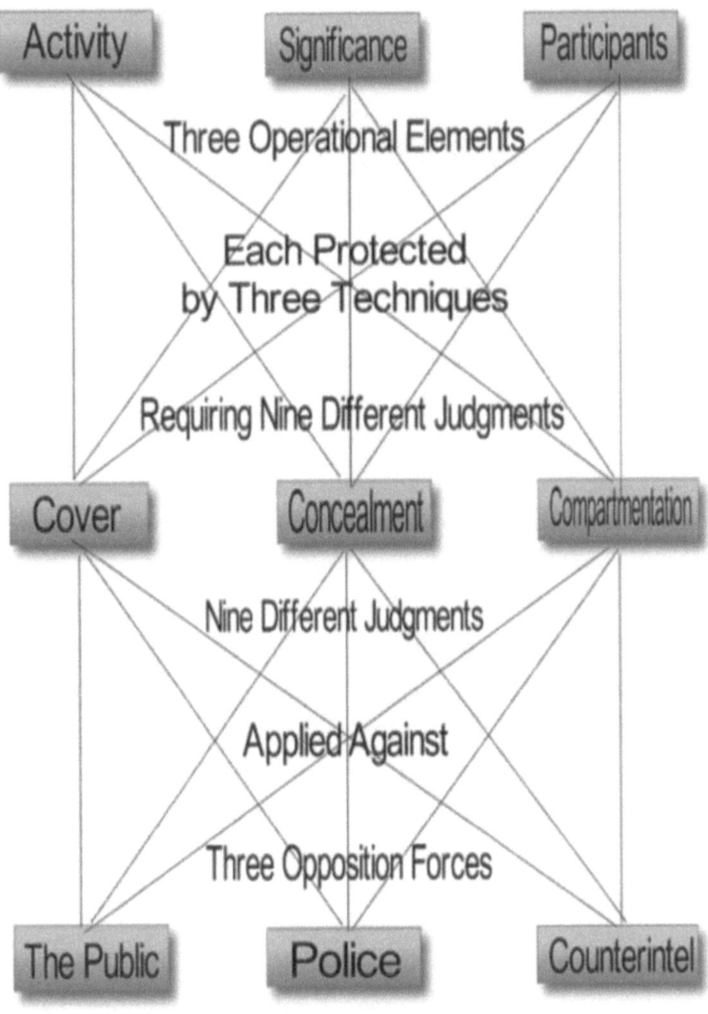

Figure 2

First of all, you are protecting them against people in general (that is, the ***public***) who often have great trust and faith in their government. Or else they fear their government. So, they are often prone to notify the authorities if they notice something strange or incongruous. In very closed societies, such incongruity might be any foreigner who is in contact with any local people.

Second, whom would they notify? Probably the police (that is, ***law enforcement*** personnel) from whom you must also protect your clandestine activities. The law enforcement authorities are not experts in clandestine operations but are often quick to spot tell-tale signs of it.

Third, law enforcement would probably refer the matter to a specialized branch of their government, that is, the ***professional counterintelligence services*** against which you must also protect your activities.

The classical way to counter the ***public, law enforcement,*** and ***professional counterintelligence services*** who threaten the ***fact, significance,*** and ***participants*** of your clandestine activity boils down to three tools: ***cover, concealment***, and ***compartmentation.*** Those who work in the espionage profession must understand these concepts well, and they must understand how entwined they are with each other.

Cover

Cover is the outward, innocent explanation for one's presence in a given country and for one's clandestine activities. Such an explanation should be as self-evident as possible so that it won't elicit questions. But if questioned, a clandestine operator or secret agent should cite a convincing explanation.

For example, if you are a clandestine operator in a foreign country, you need a **cover** for being there. The **cover** for being in a specific country is known as **status cover**. It can vary from being an engineer, a businessman, a scientific researcher, an investor, an artist, a writer of travel books, an architectural or wildlife photographer, a student, a teacher, a naturalist, a retiree, or a participant in any other convincing and innocent overt activity.

All such **cover** has to be verifiable and confirmable. This is of utmost importance. No matter how clever you are, no matter how well you think on your feet, you cannot get by with glib but unverifiable claims as to who you are or what you are doing. It might work when dealing casually with the **public,** but it is less likely to work if **law enforcement** scrutinizes you and checks up on what you say, and it certainly will not work if **professional counterintelligence** decides to investigate you.

Whatever you claim to be, there had better be a confirmation of it in your public background in case someone decides to check on you. If you claim to be a photographer or a writer you had better have a convincing record of work as a photographer or writer. If you are a student or teacher you had better be enrolled as a student, and you had better be studying seriously, or else be teaching. If you claim to be a retiree, there had better be a record of your service with an organization that sends you your retirement annuity. Crafting a verifiable **cover** is known as **backstopping**. It is a burdensome but necessary chore. The road to espionage-hell is paved with sloppy and abbreviated efforts to create cover. **Cover** takes time and effort.

Cover is necessary not only to justify your legitimate presence in a country, but to protect you when engaging in a specific clandestine act. The *cover* to justify a specific activity is known as *action cover*. Why are you going to certain part of town (where you will meet with your secret agent)? Why are you with a certain person (your agent) at all? What is your ostensible reason for hanging around a building (where you are secretly observing who goes in and out)? All these activities require *cover*, preferably a *cover* that does not evince curiosity, but which will also lend itself to a persuasive explanation.

Of course, the ideal would be never to have to rely on *cover* at all, and for all clandestine activities to be hidden. But it would be difficult to hide them completely from all three opposition forces mentioned above so that *cover* would not be necessary as a fallback. But, yes, a clandestine operator or an agent does hide all his clandestine activity to some degree, and this is where *concealment* plays a role. As we said earlier, the techniques to protect our clandestine activity are necessarily entwined.

Concealment

Concealment means physically hiding a person, an activity, or an object to make it less likely that one will ever need a *cover* story to explain it. *Concealment* is not as simple as it seems, for the very act of concealing something is suspect. So, if at all possible, *concealment* itself should have a cover explanation. Again, the principles of operational security are necessarily entwined.

Let's say you, as a male clandestine operator who is obviously a foreigner, must meet with a local female clerk-stenographer who works for the local government and is your *secret agent*.

In such a case, the incongruity of your contact might draw some attention. You might decide that the better part of wisdom is to hide your contact entirely. So, each of you gets a room in a large hotel, where the comings and goings of the guests are somewhat anonymous, and one can sneak unobserved from one's own room to the other's room to hold a meeting. Such a procedure would offer good **concealment**.

But it also requires a good ***action cover***. There must be a convincing reason as to why each of you rented a room in the hotel. Perhaps the agent came to town to visit some museum. She ought therefore to actually go to a few museums while there and purchase museum guide books. And, your own story is that you were in town to see a play or attend a conference. You ought therefore to go to see a play or actually attend a conference.

A hotel room might not be practical if the agent's outward financial situation would not lend itself to renting an expensive room in a large hotel. In such a case, the clandestine operator might have at his disposal an apartment or house which a local person who is also a ***secret agent*** rents for him, and who has a cover reason for having such premises. Such a location is known as a "safehouse," and we will discuss that concept more thoroughly later on.

And both clandestine operator and agent who meet together in a hotel or other premises should also have a ***cover*** story in case they are caught together. In such an eventuality you might, for example, claim to be lovers, which might protect the significance of your contact. To pull that off, you should each have a thorough common knowledge of your alleged relationship in case you're questioned. You must know how you allegedly first met, previous assignations, and so forth. With such preparation, you can conceal your activity and cover it at the same time.

But sometimes it is difficult to devise a **cover** story to explain why something is concealed. For example, if you have a hiding place for certain incriminating material such as stolen documents, microfilm, a clandestine radio, or code material, it would be next to impossible to concoct a **cover** story that would convince the public, or law enforcement, or the professional counterintelligence opposition that what you are doing is above-board. In such a case you might claim that you know nothing about the material, that it must belong to someone else. Although such a claim is obviously weak, one must still use it as a **cover**, and one must stick to it, howsoever implausible, if only for legal reasons which might be factors in some countries.

And, if at any time in the past you worked openly for an intelligence service (say in an administrative position or as an analyst in your home country) but now are about to work clandestinely abroad, you would have to adopt a new identity; one which bears no trace of any past intelligence affiliation. This is essential because no **cover** would work effectively against a **professional counterintelligence** opposition that would thoroughly investigate your background. If you come to their attention, they would discover your past intelligence affiliation, and would not be persuaded that you are not still on the payroll of an intelligence service. But, adopting a new identity is <u>not</u> **cover**. After all, you are not explaining who you are. You are hiding it. So, that too comes under the rubric of **concealment**.

When dealing with **concealment**, we might run straight against another critical aspect of operational security. If someone constructs a physical hiding place for your incriminating material, or if someone maintains an apartment for your use for secret meetings, or if someone provides an innocuous address for you to receive messages or signals from a clandestine contact, or if someone fabricates false identity documents for you, or if someone who is knowledgeable in your ostensible field of endeavor is asked to confirm your ostensible status, it means expanding the number of people who know of your clandestine operation, thereby reducing the protection of good **compartmentation** which is another protective tool that is often entwined with **cover** and **concealment**.

Compartmentation

Compartmentation ensures that as few people as possible know about one's clandestine activity, and that those who are aware of it are aware of only as much as necessary to carry out their role in it. It is sometimes expressed as the "Need to Know Principle," which strictly limits knowledge of secret matters to those who need to know it.

So, if crafting a **status cover,** most of which requires some kind of backstopping, it would be necessary, as mentioned above, to have the witting cooperation of people openly knowledgeable of your ostensible field of activity who could confirm your status relative to it. As we have noted, such cooperation weakens **compartmentation** by adding to the number of people who know that you are a clandestine operator. Yet, it might be unavoidable in order to have a convincing **status cover** in a given foreign country. In such a case one must limit such knowledge as much as possible, and try to ensure that the back-stopper be in a different country so he would be less subject to scrutiny or investigation by the authorities in the country where one is operating. Hence, a related factor would be concealment of detailed backstopping-data from analysis by the opposing **counterintelligence service**, which might reveal such suspicious things as low overt work output of the person under **cover**.

Or let us say, as in one of the examples mentioned above, that the very fact that your secret agent is in contact with a foreigner is so risky that you decide it would be safer to meet under **concealment** in an apartment or a house (a "safehouse" as mentioned earlier). In such a case, the person who owns or rents the house is aware that the premises are being used for a clandestine activity, and that, too, weakens **compartmentation**. So, the person who provides the premises must be carefully chosen and well-trusted, and the knowledge of the matter limited strictly to him or her. Also, **cover** is deeply entwined in the activity because, as mentioned earlier, there must be a **cover** reason for you and your agent to be in such a place.

One of the most common aspects running through the history of espionage is the comparative advantage of running a series of agents individually who are unaware of each other and thus well-compartmented, rather than running a network of agents who know of each other and can therefore communicate more efficiently among themselves, thereby creating different channels for the flow of information. Here we see a trade-off between efficiency and security. In a later chapter on counterintelligence we will underscore the danger of networks, and their vulnerability to the **professional counterintelligence opposition**.

When All is Said and Done

In the foregoing paragraphs we have shown that whenever we engage in clandestine activity, the various elements of operational security interact with each other, even if we must analyze the elements separately.

Since there are three things that must be protected from three types of opposition through three different methods, a good security analysis of a clandestine activity requires, as we have already pointed out, twenty-seven different interactions that a clandestine operator should constantly consider.

The basic principles of operational security outlined in this chapter point to an ideal of operational perfection. But to be realistic, the exigencies of the real world, the need for results, and the pressures of time will always force the clandestine operator to skimp on one aspect or other.

Cover is never air-tight. **Concealment** is never perfect. And there will always be a lack of perfect **Compartmentation**. Often a clandestine operator will truncate the application of one or more of these protective tools in order to enhance the application of another. The degree to which a clandestine operator applies each of the principles of operational security is always a matter of judgment, which becomes fine-tuned with experience.

The balance that one seeks lies somewhere between total efficiency on one side, and total security on the other. <u>Total efficiency</u> would allow a clandestine operator to operate frequently, swiftly and openly, without any delays or obstacles stemming from concealment, cover, and compartmentation. But such a situation is devoid of <u>security</u>. On the other hand, <u>total</u>

<u>security</u> would require one to take no risks and, therefore, carry out no clandestine activity at all, which would mean no <u>efficiency</u> whatsoever, and would yield no results.

Certainly, a successful practitioner of human source espionage or covert action might aspire to operational perfection, but he must recognize that it is impossible to achieve complete perfection if he is to have any results. The principles of operational security outlined in this chapter are a framework to guide the thinking of a clandestine operator, but cannot prescribe any absolutes regarding cover, concealment, or compartmentation. On the other hand, these principles should generate a mentality that, in due course, becomes instinctive in those who practice spycraft. (Figure 3).

SECURITY versus EFFICIENCY
- A Trade-Off -

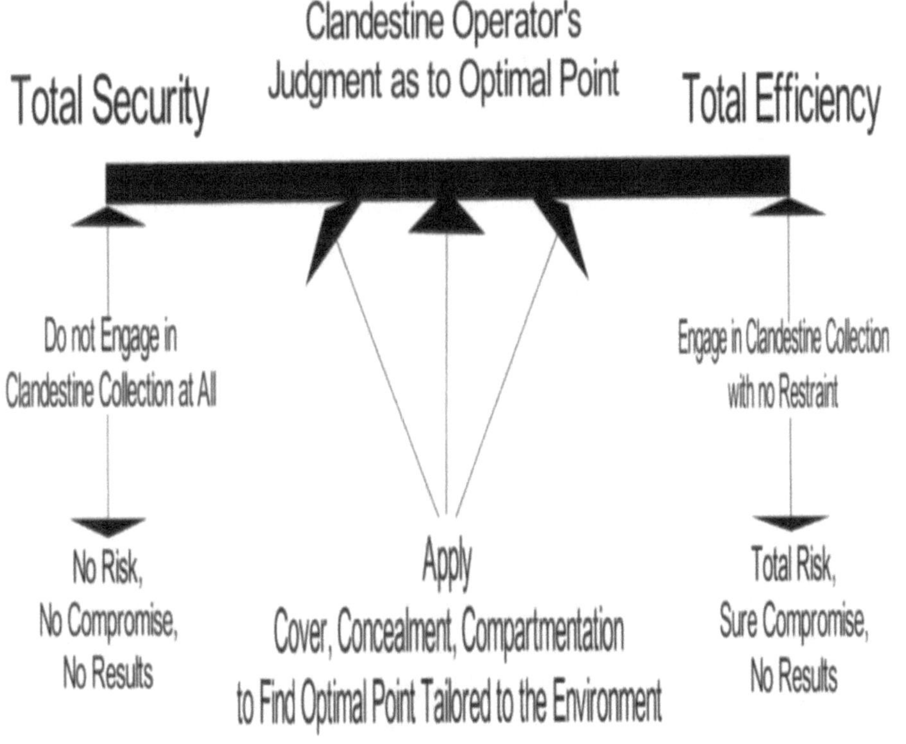

Figure 3

CHAPTER II

Agent Acquisition

Where and how do clandestine organizations get their secret agents? They either recruit them or else the agents are volunteers. Before we recruit such agents, we must search for them. And before we search for them, we must have a clear understanding of what we want from them, and this is also true before we accept even a volunteer into the fold.

Qualifications of a Secret Agent

The qualifications we seek in a secret agent can vary considerably. Of course, one of the ultimate goals of the clandestine operator's sponsor (that is, the clandestine organization) is to acquire agents who can report non-public information of interest to its customers (that is, to government analysts and policy-makers), or to carry out secret activities in support of those customers. In such cases, the key qualification of a secret agent is his access to such information or else access to power and influence. The salient qualification is always <u>access</u>. In seeking non-public information, an agent who is situated as a legitimate member of an organization where he has access to material that the sponsor seeks is often called an **agent in place,** or a **penetration** of that organization.

There are also many alternate qualifications of a secret agent - qualifications that do not require access to information or power. For example, we might need a secret agent who can do certain things for us such as procure rental cars without indicating that they are for us, or who can provide a house or apartment for us without others knowing that it is for us. Or an agent who can act as a messenger or courier between a clandestine operator and an agent who does have access to information of interest to policy makers. Or an agent at an airport or train station who can keep an eye out for us as to conditions in those places and report who comes and goes. Or an agent who can provide a mailing address for us, thereby concealing our association with that address. Or agents who can work as a team to carry out surveillance on our behalf. Or an agent in the local police who can perform investigations for us under cover of his legitimate police authority without anyone else knowing that it's for us. We might even want to recruit agents whose job is to spot other potential agents whom we might try to recruit later.

Not to be ignored under the rubric of "qualifications" are some of the agent's personal qualities. He must be knowledgeable and intelligent enough to do the job. If he reports on political and economic matters, he must be able to grasp and express those disciplines. If he is going to tap local telephones for us, he must have the requisite technical know-how to do it. He must be responsible enough to follow instructions regarding such things as contact arrangements and personal security. If he is unstable, or a drunkard, or downright dumb, one must balance his value versus the risk of using him.

Another aspect to bear in mind regarding a secret agent is his personal security. Has he been in trouble with the police? Does he attract too much unnecessary attention? Has anybody on the opposing side ever questioned his security? Is he likely to come under the scrutiny of the law enforcement or professional opposition which might lead them to discover his ties to your own clandestine organization?

Nevertheless, none of the qualifications has any significance whatsoever unless the agent is willing to work for you, and that leads us to the all-important factor of motivation.

Motivation

Why would someone want to work as a secret agent at great risk to himself? Motivation, along with an agent's qualifications, is one of the two most important questions when seeking a new agent. The list of possible motivations is almost endless.

It can be for ideological, cultural, or racial affinity with the sponsor and the sponsor's country. It can be for a deep opposition to a hateful regime in his own country, and a sense that by cooperating with the sponsor he is actually being a patriot. It can be for personal attachments of some sort or other

Motivation can also be less lofty. It can range from ego-gratification, self-image, greed, revenge, the need for friendship and appreciation, and reciprocal favors. Among the latter might be medical treatment for a loved one, eventual exfiltration out of one's country, strings pulled for career advancement, desire for excitement, and other mundane reasons. Sometimes it is merely the result of threats and coercion.

Spotting Potential Agents and Reporting on Them

Sometimes a potential agent takes the initiative and offers himself as a volunteer to a potential sponsor (and this will be discussed later), but in most cases a clandestine organization must recruit its agents. The recruitment is best done by clandestine operators who work for the sponsoring organization. The clandestine operators are the communication link between the sponsor and the agents, and they manage the activities of the agents.

Occasionally secret agents recruit other agents, but it is generally not a good idea for those agents who enjoy useful access to information or to power to know the identities of other agents, or to expose themselves by attempting to recruit others. It is dangerous, and it blatantly violates the principle of compartmentation.

Of course, a clandestine operator who works for a sponsoring clandestine organization should have extensive training to understand what is expected of a secret agent. The operator must be skilled in discerning a secret agent's motivation and abilities, and in understanding whether the agent is capable of fulfilling the needs of his organization.

The clandestine operator whose job is to carry out agent recruitments must have a cover and a personality that is conducive to meeting and socializing with a broad spectrum of people in the environment where he lives and works. And he must be an excellent "people person" with the added dimension of keen psychological insight and cross-cultural understanding.

<u>It is an iron rule of clandestine operations that an operator must report to his organization all of his significant clandestine activities including his search for new agents. The purpose is not only to receive guidance and tutelage from his superiors, but also to establish a record of his operations in case of discovery and compromise.</u>

In the case of discovery or compromise, his own organization's counterintelligence elements will review all aspects of what happened beforehand in order to assess not only the reasons for the compromise, but the extent of the damage in terms of what the opposition learned from it. Another reason for submitting reports is that the greatest single asset of any sponsoring intelligence organization is its accumulated files with names, places, topics and locations carefully indexed and retrievable through an index search. We will discuss this in a later chapter.

When a clandestine operator or an agent submits a report as part of a search for a new agent, we might call it an "agent search report" or perhaps a "spotting report." There is no set format for such reporting, and it varies from organization to organization. Obviously it will contain identifying information as to the spotter and his target. In addition, it will contain a preliminary and abbreviated judgment of the subject's qualifications and potential usefulness to the clandestine organization, as well as his possible motivation to perform such work - that is, all the elements already emphasized above. It would also be helpful for the report to include information as to the target's personal characteristics, and of course any security considerations that might have a bearing on further contact with him.

A Hypothetical Scenario

To better understand the foregoing, let us set up a hypothetical scenario. Assume that your country's sponsoring clandestine organization employs one of its own citizens who is a vigorous, sharp, and well-trained clandestine operator who lives and works under good status cover in the Republic of Probahlia. To protect the operator's identity, we will refer to him by a pseudonym, SHARPERSON.

SHARPERSON's mission is to search for, assess, and eventually recruit sources of non-public information on Probahlia and its government. It is a difficult task because relations between Probahlia and SHARPERSON's own country are somewhat cool, and Probahlian citizens, especially those in government with access to the information that SHARPERSON seeks, keep him at arm's length.

But let's say that at the local International Club, SHARPERSON meets a certain Samilo Dravunio Hembersol, who is a major in the air force of a nearby country called Degenera, and is serving in the air attache's office in the Degeneran Embassy in Probahlia. Since Degenera and Probahlia have good relations, SHARPERSON assesses Hembersol as a potential source on Probahlian affairs, and perhaps eventually as a source on Hembersol's home country, Degenera, which is also an information-collection target of SHARPERSON's clandestine organization.

SHARPERSON and Hembersol develop a social relationship. As two foreigners living in a third country, their social contact attracts little or no interest either by the public, or local law enforcement, or the local (Probahlian) professional counterintelligence opposition. In the course of their relationship,

SHARPERSON elicits from Hembersol that the Degeneran air force sent him abroad as an attache to get him out of the way because of his criticism of Degeneran military policy and because of some of his expressed misgivings regarding activities of the Degeneran government back home. The foregoing raises the possibility of political disaffection on Hembersol's part, and perhaps points to his eventual "recruitability." SHARPERSON also notes Hembersol's open and gregarious personality, his hobbies and interests (he loves chess, for example), his ease in international circles, and his affinity for people of SHARPERSON's nationality.

In due course SHARPERSON will submit an agent search report delineating everything he has learned about Hembersol as a potential agent, noting his qualifications in terms of his access to information of interest, and also his potential motivation. We should emphasize, however, that such an agent-search report is essentially a preliminary document. If the sponsoring clandestine organization agrees that the individual might be of potential use and might be "recruitable" as a secret agent, the clandestine organization will observe him further, not only through direct contact, but also through investigation and research.

Investigating Potential Agents

Let us say in the foregoing hypothetical scenario that SHARPERSON's clandestine organization decides that indeed, on the basis of clandestine operator SHARPERSON's search report, that Major Samilo Dravunio Hembersol, is worthy of future scrutiny as a recruitment target. So, the very next step would be to investigate Hembersol.

Such an investigation would start with a check of the clandestine organization's file holdings containing countless documents whose contents are indexed for later retrievability (more on files in a later chapter). After all, who knows if Hembersol appears in other documents and in other contexts in past years. All of the foregoing would be combined with publicly-available information found, perhaps, in the media or elsewhere in the holdings of the clandestine organization's own customer.

Let us say that one of the organization's agents who works in Degenera's military personnel office had in the past included Hembersol's name in a reported list of graduates of the Degeneran Military Academy, thus confirming Hembersol's elite background. And that the agent also reported that a few years later, Hembersol was one of several young officers who completed flight training and earned his wings as a fighter pilot. But another agent, who was a low-level administrative clerk in the Degeneran Air Force, reported that subsequently, Hembersol crashed his plane, that a court of inquiry ruled that the crash was the result of pilot error, and had recommended that Hembersol no longer be permitted to fly.

The clandestine organization might then query existing agents for additional information, and might even put Hembersol under surveillance to compile information about his activities and lifestyle that might help to better understand him. Note, however, that the decision to query other secret agents about Hembersol, or to put him under surveillance requires due consideration as to the loss of compartmentation accruing from the knowledge afforded to others of the clandestine organization's interest in him.

Remembering that Hembersol once commented to clandestine operator SHARPERSON that he disagreed with certain aspects of the Degeneran governing regime, SHARPERSON's clandestine organization asks another clandestine operator - one who works in Degenera - to query a long-time and trusted agent who is a senior official of the ruling People's Democratic Party (PDP) about Hembersol. In order not to flag the clandestine organization's particular interest in Hembersol, the clandestine operator in Degenera mixed the request for information on Hembersol with requests for information on a dozen other Degenerans serving in the Degeneran Embassy in Probahlia, thereby making the query about Hembersol seem like a routine broad request without undue significance. The agent in Degenera then noted that Hembersol's family are long-time PDP loyalists and that Hembersol's father pulled strings to get his son the plush assignment in the military attache's office in the Degeneran Embassy in Probahlia.

At this point, Hembersol seems to SHARPERSON and to his clandestine sponsoring organization to be a worthy candidate for recruitment. Not only does the investigation confirm his qualifications as a possible source on Probahlia where he is currently assigned, but once he returns to his home country, he will also have direct access to information on the Degeneran Air Force and possibly the Degeneran People's Democratic Party through his family. We recall that he has confided to SHAPERSON that he is somewhat critical of the Degeneran Air Force and the Degeneran political regime, thus signaling possible susceptibilities to recruitment. Last, his disqualification as a pilot, which was undoubtedly damaging to a career as an aviator, might of course add to his disaffection, and contribute to a future motivation to work for SHARPERSON.

Assessing and Developing

Often the clandestine operator who will eventually attempt the recruitment is the same spotter who knows the individual and had initial access to him. At other times the spotter might be a local agent embedded in place with unique access to people with agent potential, rather than a foreigner like clandestine operator SHARPERSON. Any eventual recruitment would pose some risks to the recruiter if the target should refuse the recruitment and then report the attempt to his own security services. So, if the spotter is particularly valuable and well-placed as an agent, it might be wise for someone else to contrive to meet the target and carry out the succeeding steps in the recruitment process.

However, in this particular case, SHARPERSON's clandestine organization decides that SHARPERSON, who has already hit it off personally with Hembersol, should begin to intensify his personal relationship with him, learn more about him, and perhaps eventually perform the actual recruitment.

So SHARPERSON deliberately runs into Hembersol more and more frequently at the International Club, and uses his "people skills" to establish yet closer rapport with him. They have drinks and lunch together, enjoy each other's company, and they become good friends. Occasionally they get together with their wives for dinner at each other's homes.

The development of a truly close personal relationship can be slow, and may even take a couple of years. Operator SHARPERSON must be patient and must spend a great deal of time with his target. He and Hembersol must confide in each other. SHARPERSON must always be there for Hembersol, always trustworthy, always on time, and never appear flaky or stupid. He must come across as a person who respects Hembersol and admires him. At the same time, he himself must come across as a person who is to be admired himself, a person on whom Hembersol can lean, and whom he can trust. SHARPERSON should appear to have a certain degree of influence or wealth, possibly through his position in his cover organization.

Clandestine operator SHARPERSON and his target Hembersol must be willing to do favors for each other. Perhaps SHARPERSON can find some household items, such as a top-of-the-line refrigerator or a television set, or a personal computer at a particularly low wholesale price which Hembersol will eventually take back to his home in Degenera. Or maybe SHARPERSON can arrange for Hembersol to convert his salary into local currency at an unusually favorable black-market rate, or else do it himself.

Sometimes the favors can be more serious. Perhaps Hembersol finds himself in some sort of debt, in which case SHARPERSON might give him a loan. Or Hembersol might find himself in a bind of some sort. Perhaps he contracts a sexually-transmitted disease from a prostitute, but he wants to keep it secret and is therefore afraid to go to a local physician to get cured. So SHARPERSON arranges for a trusted physician-friend of his to clear up the infection.

And SHARPERSON can ask for favors too. He might say that his company needs some background on the Probahlian military, perhaps regarding its leadership, some aspects of its corporate culture, or perhaps information on a given Probahlian military officer, for which information SHARPERSON can then express gratitude and appreciation. The important thing is the development of a close interactive relationship of confidence and trust.

During this time SHARPERSON will try to refine his assessment of his target, and will give particular attention to learning two important aspects of his character. These are Hembersol's ***susceptibilities*** and Hembersol's ***vulnerabilities***, which in the espionage profession are separate and different traits which deserve careful probing.

Susceptibilities and Vulnerabilities

Susceptibilities are those things that might motivate a prospective secret agent to attach himself closer and closer to the clandestine operator who is developing a relationship with him, and perhaps lead to his eventual willingness to become a secret agent on his behalf. For example:

Hembersol might have at some point confided in SHARPERSON about financial difficulties, or indicated a certain personal venality. Or else, operator SHARPERSON might have detected in Hembersol a certain need for ego gratification, and SHARPERSON might have allowed himself to be impressed by Hembersol's continuous bragging. Or perhaps Hembersol might have indicated a certain resentment towards his own country's regime for moral or ideological reasons despite his family's traditional loyalty towards it. Or possibly Hembersol might feel bitterness in having been passed over for promotion, or a sense of unfairness regarding his limited future in the Degeneran Air Force stemming from the crashing of his plane which Hembersol characterized as an unfortunate mishap not at all his fault. All these personal feelings represent susceptibilities to be manipulated psychologically.

Vulnerabilities are different from susceptibilities. Vulnerabilities are those negative things about a person that he would not want others to know, particularly his superiors or his government, or members of his society or his family, but which he shares with clandestine operator SHARPERSON who will be his eventual recruiter. And there are good reasons that a clandestine operator might want to know negative information about his recruitment target.

Any shared knowledge between the clandestine operator and the potential secret agent adds to the trust between the two people. But more important, the shared knowledge of vulnerabilities protects the clandestine operator as well as the sponsoring clandestine organization and its customers. How? Of great immediate importance is if a prospective agent should reject an eventual offer of recruitment, he would be less tempted to go to the authorities to report it if there is a real danger that some unsavory information might emerge regarding himself. Also, if your prospective agent has vulnerabilities, you want to know about them before someone else instead decides to use them to blackmail him.

I have known a number of operational supervisors (including me) who refused to allow their subordinates to attempt recruitments unless they had acquired vulnerability information regarding their targets that would to some degree preclude any "blowback" in case their recruitment efforts failed

Activity Reports

As clandestine operator SHARPERSON develops his relationship with Hembersol, he will submit reports on every single contact he has with him. These may be called "activity reports" or "contact reports." <u>As mentioned earlier, it is essential in well-managed clandestine operations to report all operational activity.</u>

The reasons are worth reviewing. First it compels the operator to review the operation in his own mind. Second, it allows operational supervisors to review the activities of their subordinates and provide supervision and tutelage. Third, if an operation ever goes sour, it will be necessary to go back and review all its historical aspects in order to pinpoint the reasons and to assess any damage to the sponsoring organization's own security.

I cannot exaggerate the importance of activity reports which, among other things, should record the time and place of a contact, its duration, security aspects and precautions, mood and attitude of the interlocutor, and any new information that might affect the progress of a case.

Such reports make a record of any changes in the subject's demeanor or attitude, and any deviations from the norm in the operational environment. They should contain any data regarding the contact's family life, personal problems, or relationship with the case officer. In short, it should contain anything that transpires that could be relevant to the operation's success or failure, now or in the future.

Activity Reports should be informal documents in which the operator not only writes down what happened, but "thinks out loud," and includes his gut feelings about the relationship. Later, these facts and feelings can be summarized in a formal periodic report to the clandestine organization's headquarters for indexing and filing. But the informal activity reports are for immediate scrutiny and for use by the office in the field, in addition to being useful much later if the situation requires it.

During the early phase of a recruitment operation, all activity reports that delineate a clandestine operator's meetings with a prospective secret agent would emphasizes the factors described earlier relating to the possible eventual recruitment of that agent. The report would, of course, identify the meeting participants, the time, and place, and the circumstances of the meeting such as a dinner together at a local restaurant in Probahlia. If their wives are present, the report would of course cite that as well.

There should be notations of <u>anything</u> that might later even tangentially affect the security of their contact, such as running into someone one or both of them know, or if SHARPERSON suspects he might be under surveillance. At this stage, since SHARPERSON's contact with Hembersol is on the up-and-up, such incidents would pose no serious problem, but they might become significant if recalled later - after Hembersol is recruited as an agent - so they MUST be reported. If nothing untoward occurs, it would also be helpful if SHARPERSON specifically states that he noted nothing unusual security-wise, and perhaps make such security-related comments that the restaurant is off the beaten track, that it is unlikely that anyone would remember their having been there, and so forth.

The activity report should obviously contain a summary of any discussion between SHARPERSON and Hembersol regarding official economic or political matters, and personal matters as well. Let us say that in this fictional case Hembersol confided to SHARPERSON that his tour of duty in Probahlia, which will be up in one year, is not being renewed or extended, and that he will be posted back to his home country of Degenera.

Specifically, he will be assigned to Degenera's High General Staff as aide to General Martisto who has been named chief of air operations. Hembersol might also have told SHARPERSON that he received this desirable assignment because General Martisto is a close friend of Hembersol's father, both having been strong supporters and activists for the ruling People's Democratic Party (PDP) in their youth.

The foregoing information is extremely relevant in assessing Hembersol's potential value as a recruited agent. In the short run (for one year) Hembersol's usefulness would be primarily as a foreign diplomat assigned to Probahlia, reporting to SHARPERSON on Probahlian affairs, but it will not be lost on SHARPERSON and his sponsoring clandestine organization that eventually, back in Degenera, Hembersol will have access to non-public information regarding the Degeneran military establishment.

Of further interest, Hembersol might confide privately to his close friend SHARPERSON, perhaps while the wives are talking separately, that he is concerned about the financial aspects of his return to Degenera, since he will no longer be earning the same overseas allowances and emoluments as during his assignment to Probahlia. Perhaps Hembersol cites medical expenses necessary for one of his children who has a club foot and needs surgery and therapy, or that his wife is pregnant and there will then be another child to support. Such information, included in activity reports, is extremely important because it goes very much towards assessing Hembersol's possible future financial motivation as an agent working for SHARPERSON's clandestine organization.

Let us also say that during the dinner, Hembersol mentions to SHARPERSON that a high-level Probahlian military officer told him that certain specific Probahlian military officers are being reassigned because the government has learned that these officers are disaffected as a result of Probahlian government policies. Hembersol asks SHARPERSON not to tell anyone that the information had come from him because it is off-the-record. SHARPERSON would later record the information briefly in his activity report, and might also submit the information separately as an information report (which will be described later in this book).

In order for SHARPERSON's supervisors to better follow SHARPERSON's social and personal relationship with Hembersol and provide advice and tutelage, SHARPERSON would include in his activity-report his plans for his future development of Hembersol, and specify the time and place of their next get-together.

Since Hembersol has now begun revealing some off-the-record information to SHARPERSON and is now a serious recruitment target, SHARPERSON's clandestine organization might, for security reasons, assign him a code name so that he can no longer be identified in future operational reporting about him. Let us assume in this case that Hembersol is now called HOPEWARS/1. The identification of HOPEWARS/1 as Hembersol will be available only in sensitive files in the sponsoring clandestine organization's headquarters.

After several similar social contacts, SHARPERSON might now judge that the time has come to try to recruit HOPEWARS/1, to get him into a more formal relationship, to establish a business-like aspect to the relationship, to get him accustomed to receiving earnings and favors, and to give him some training in clandestinity before turning him over for eventual handling by a different clandestine operator in Degenera after HOPEWARS/1 is reassigned back there.

Character Studies or Assessment Reports

SHARPERSON now submits to his superiors a full character study of HOPEWARS/1, assessing him thoroughly as to his "recruitability." Such a character-study would be very much like an agent-search report or spotting report, but much more detailed, as it would contain much information that SHARPERSON has developed about HOPEWARS/1 over a long period—perhaps a couple of years - of increasingly close social interaction.

SHARPERSON would strongly emphasize the dual potential usefulness and qualifications of HOPEWARS/1, which in this case would be the access he enjoys to the military establishment of Probahlia where HOPEWARS/1 is assigned, and his obvious access to Degeneran military matters once he is reassigned back home. SHARPERSON might even call attention to HOPEWARS/1's potential for rising in the Degeneran Air Force to a position of influence, even if not as an aviator for having once crashed his plane. In addition, SHARPERSON would mention the prominence of HOPEWARS/1's family in Degenera's ruling People's Democratic Party (PDS), and the possibility that HOPEWARS/1 could also become a source on the Party itself.

HOPEWARS/1's <u>susceptibility</u> to recruitment would be a key item in SHARPERSON's assessment of him. SHARPERSON knows that HOPEWARS/1 is in dire need of money because, on occasion, he told SHARPERSON about certain debts he contracted back in Degenera and his concerns about providing for the future of his child. HOPEWARS/1 has become accustomed to SHARPERSON's willingness to convert HOPEWARS/1's monthly salary to local currency at an advantageous rate. Also, despite HOPEWARS/1's family's strong association with the PDP, HOPEWARS/1 has expressed disdain for the PDP's fascist ideology and for the corruption within PDP ranks. Last, HOPEWARS/1 feels bitter about his treatment by the Degeneran Air Force hierarchy which has removed him from the ranks of flight officers for having been involved in a freak flying accident which HOPEWARS/1 insists was not his fault. Further to HOPEWARS/1's susceptibility, clandestine operator SHARPERSON has characterized HOPEWARS/1 as a somewhat spoiled scion of an important family, with a big ego and a somewhat exaggerated sense of his own importance which SHARPERSON believes makes HOPEWARS/1 "manipulatable."

But in order for SHARPERSON to get a green light to attempt to recruit HOPEWARS/1, SHARPERSON must (as we mentioned earlier in this book) delineate HOPEWARS/1's <u>vulnerabilities</u> that would discourage HOPEWARS/1 from reporting any recruitment attempt to his superiors. In the character study, SHARPERSON would reiterate that HOPEWARS/1 has engaged in illegal currency transactions that yielded him a significantly higher exchange rate than normally available, and if known could signal the end of his career. Also, HOPEWARS/1 is something of a womanizer, and SHARPERSON has arranged for him to receive treatment "on the quiet" for a sexually transmitted disease that HOPEWARS/1 caught from a prostitute in Probahlia. HOPEWARS/1 has also supplied SHARPERSON with some "don't-tell-anyone-I told-you" information which, if known to HOPEWARS/1's supervisors, could cause him immense trouble.

SHARPERSON would also note security factors attending any recruitment of HOPEWARS/1. Of course, their acquaintance is known in the Probahlian international community, although the depth of their friendship might not be apparent because SHARPERSON has many other visible friends as well. The indiscretions committed by HOPEWARS/1 and which HOPEWARS/1 has shared with SHARPERSON could conceivably also make HOPEWARS/1 attractive to others, so if the clandestine organization recruits HOPEWARS/1 it will have to train him seriously in security matters. Fortunately, HOPEWARS/1's indiscretions, his need for money, and his disaffection with both his government and with the Degeneran Air Force, have probably not yet come to the attention of the Degeneran security authorities, probably because HOPEWARS/1 has been serving abroad these past few years.

Also, in the area of security, SHARPERSON would emphasize that a recruitment attempt of HOPEWARS/1 would carry diminished risk if it comes to the attention of HOPEWARS/1's counterintelligence services in Degenera because the recruitment would be slanted to SHARPERSON's interest in Probahlia rather than HOPEWARS/1's own country of Degenera. The foregoing would lessen any damage in the relations between SHARPERSON's country and Degenera if by chance HOPEWARS/1 were to report the recruitment attempt to his superiors. It is only later, when HOPEWARS/1 becomes more accustomed to his role as an agent for SHARPERSON against Probahlia, that SHARPERSON may be able to ease him into reporting useful information on Degenera itself.

Another factor to be mentioned is that SHARPERSON and HOPEWARS/1 have known each other for a long time, are friends, and thanks to SHARPERSON's long patience, it is somewhat less likely that HOPEWARS/1 will consider that SHARPERSON was manipulating him and leading him down the garden path for two whole years, even though that is precisely what has been going on. (As I said at the outset of this book, human source espionage is a sleazy activity, and it does require much time and patience.)

At this point, SHARPERSON's superiors will decide (see Figure 4) whether to approve a formal recruitment attempt of Major Samilo Dravunio Hembersol (referred to as HOPEWARS/1), of the Degeneran Air Force, currently a military attache in the Degeneran Embassy in Probahlia, and who is scheduled to return to Degenera in one year at the conclusion of his tour of duty.

Recruiting

Assuming that SHARPERSON'S superiors give the green light for a recruitment attempt, the scenario might unfold in a number of different ways depending on the style of the clandestine operator and requisites of cover and security. A typical scenario might be as follows:

Let us say that during one of their meetings, HOPEWARS/1 mentions his financial problems once again. He bemoans his impending return to Degenera in one year, after which he will no longer have the allowances and benefits he currently enjoys as an attache posted in his country's embassy overseas. "I've been able to save a bit during this tour," he told operator SHARPERSON, "but not enough to give me a good cushion when I am re-assigned back home." SHARPERSON is aware that HOPEWARS/1 is somewhat venal and a spendthrift (which is the reason he has been unable to build a financial "cushion"), so SHARPERSON takes the following approach:

DECISION TO RECRUIT

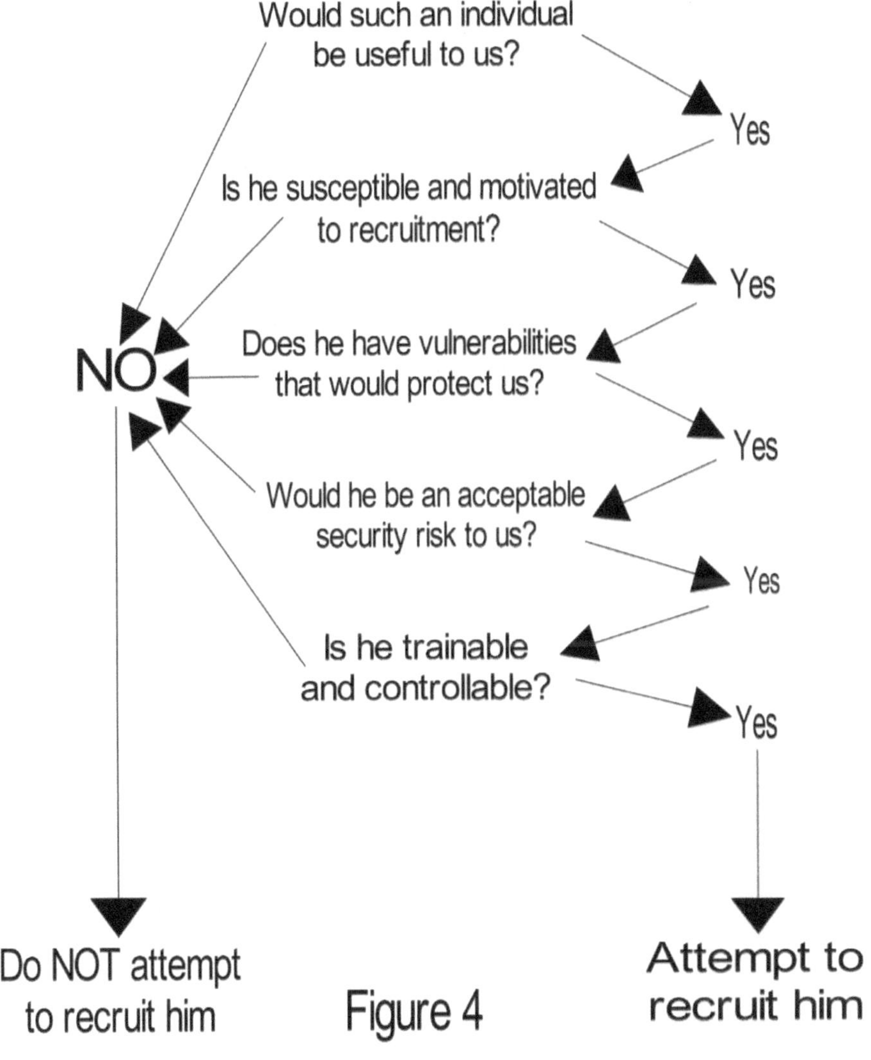

Figure 4

"Gee, Samilo, you and I have been good friends for a couple of years now. We're comfortable with each other, and we've helped each other on occasion. You've mentioned financial problems several times before, and I've been thinking of ways in which I might help. It occurs to me that I have a budget for my work (whatever cover SHARPERSON is living under in Probahlia) with an ample slush fund for public relations and the acquisition of local information. As you know, my country does not have good relations with Probahlia, so it is somewhat difficult for me to make significant contacts here. However, your country, Degenera, has excellent and close relations with Probahlia, and you, as a Degeneran military officer, have many doors open to you and are welcome as a close contact with significant Probahlian personalities. You've helped me in the past by explaining Probahlian matters to me, but if you would supply me regularly with your observations and opinions regarding Probahlia, and regarding Probahlian individuals whom you know, as well as any other information that you acquire regarding events in the Probahlian military, government, and business community, I could probably justify giving you, say, $1,000 a month every month during your final year here until you return to Degenera. I could even justify giving you a $1,000 bonus up-front, so when you return to Degenera you will have accumulated $13,000!!"

At this point, HOPEWARS/1 might ask who would know about such a relationship, and SHARPERSON would reply "Nobody. In fact, let's create a fictitious name for you to which I'll attribute the information you give me, so you'll really be quite anonymous. Nobody will know who you are except me."

Ideally, HOPEWARS/1 will agree to an arrangement of this kind. And, in order to get him into the new relationship right away, operator SHARPERSON will ask HOPEWARS/1 for his observations regarding some Probahlian military contact whom HOPEWARS/1 has dealt with. He will subsequently hand HOPEWARS/1 $1,000.00 as an initial "bonus." If possible, SHARPERSON will ask HOPEWARS/1 to sign a receipt, since "my funds need to be accounted for," but HOPEWARS/1 can sign it in any anonymous alias he chooses. While a signed receipt is not actually necessary, it does establish a certain business-like formality to the clandestine relationship which will serve in good stead as the relationship eventually becomes more and more solidified and professional. All the foregoing will be contained in the activity report describing the recruitment.

By having HOPEWARS/1 sign a receipt, SHARPERSON not only introduces a business-like atmosphere into the relationship, but by allowing HOPEWARS/1 to do it in alias, also introduces a new element of clandestinity and security. While not wanting to put too much emphasis on secrecy at this early stage lest it scares off the new recruit, SHARPERSON might still suggest that it might be a good idea that in the future they not socialize together so openly as in the past and not discuss these matters on the telephone. In fact, SHARPERSON could say that it might be better not even to arrange meetings over the phone at all, and instead arrange their next meeting right then and there. SHARPERSON might also suggest that HOPEWARS/1 not tell his wife because people sometimes let things slip out inadvertently. (All the foregoing falls into the category of new-agent-training, which SHARPERSON will carry out bit-by-bit over the succeeding months.) During their meeting, SHARPERSON asks HOPEWARS/1 to think of a way to explain his new money to his wife, but HOPEWARS/1 says that he handles all the finances in the family and she doesn't have a clue about it. As for bringing such money back to Degenera,

HOPEWARS/1 noted that all officials assigned abroad bring money back with them, so it wouldn't raise eyebrows.

There are many alternatives to the foregoing recruitment scenario. If SHARPERSON wants to create some sort of personal deniability to protect his own cover, he can say at the outset, "Gee, Samilo, you've mentioned financial problems before, and I've been thinking of ways in which I might help. I do know a guy who is attached to my country's intelligence service and I know those guys are loaded with money that they are willing to toss around in exchange for information on Probahlian military and government personalities. I don't like to get involved in such things, but as a good friend I can arrange a meeting if you wish." If HOPEWARS/1 agrees, operator SHARPERSON can then wheel out another clandestine operator, perhaps flown in from Degenera or another country, to act as the heavy and make the final recruitment pitch.

SHARPERSON's activity report of the recruitment meeting will, as usual, identify the participants in the interaction, the date and place, and comments as to any security issues or lack of security issues attendant on the meeting itself. It should also record the arrangement for their next meeting, including their cover for seeing each other (at this stage, simple social cover) and the concealment of their meeting (an out of the way restaurant or bar). The activity report should make a record of all such elements, howsoever innocuous, for reasons already given earlier in this book.

Despite all the protocols, safeguards, procedures, and analysis outlined so far, the recruitment of a new agent abroad, where the recruiting organization does not have full control of the environment, is always a risky activity. When done successfully, it will always result in some form of jubilation, and career-enhancing plaudits for the recruiter.

Standard Procedure for Agent Acquisition

As the reader might discern from all the foregoing, the recruitment of a new agent is always a risky activity. But, as the reader might also discern, there is a definite series of steps in the recruitment process which, if followed carefully, would diminish the risk and preclude the clandestine operator from going blindly and mindlessly into the attempt.

So, to reiterate, after spotting a potential recruitment target, the clandestine operator must investigate him. As mentioned, the investigation is done through file checks, reference to overt information, local queries of established agents (tempered by the need for compartmentation), and perhaps even by monitoring his activities by surveillance.

Then the clandestine operator must assess the target, which he does through patient contact over a prolonged period. Concurrent with the assessment of the potential agent is the careful development of a relationship which would culminate in a recruitment offer. (Figure 5).

What a clandestine organization must NOT do is plunge into a relationship without heeding these necessary steps. A recruitment offer is a serious act which can backfire strongly against the clandestine operator, his organization, and his organization's sponsor.

Volunteers or "Walk-Ins

Although one must usually expend a lot of time and energy to lead a prospective agent "down the garden path," towards recruitment, some agent acquisitions seem much easier, at least on the surface. These are people who approach clandestine organizations on their own initiative, or seek out offices of the customer organization to volunteer their services as spies. The western powers during the Cold War acquired some of its most valuable agents that way.

Despite the apparent ease of such an agent acquisition, the procedures for integrating a "volunteer" agent into a clandestine organization's espionage system is also very time-consuming and complex, even if somewhat different than when one laboriously develops an individual towards eventual recruitment. Let's consider a scenario in which, say, Vladero Daphnic, an employee in the Embassy of the Republic of Totalituzzia, attempts to contact a clandestine organization of another country to offer his services.

Whoever first receives Daphnic's approach would probably refer him to someone experienced in handling such matters. Care must be taken because sometimes an opposition clandestine organization might deliberately send someone as an ostensible volunteer to try to identify any clandestine operators who would handle the situation systematically and professionally. One camouflage to counter such an effort is for the interviewer to whom the volunteer is eventually referred to read off questions from a form, indicating that the questions are a standard procedure that ANY interviewer must follow.

ACQUISTION OF SECRET AGENTS
- Five Step Sequence -

1) Spotting

Directly by Clandestine Operator
and/or by Secret Agents

2) Investigating

File Check, Inquiries, Monitoring

3) Assessing

Direct Contact with Clandestine Operator
and/or with Secret Agents

4) Developing

Direct Contact
with Clandestine Operator

5) Recruiting

By Clandestine Operator

Can be Done Together

Can be Done Together

Figure 5

Whoever finally interviews Daphnic will face the delicate and difficult task of compiling an assessment report on him without the benefit of a long association that a clandestine operator would enjoy when developing a personal relationship with a potential agent. Common sense dictates that the interviewer should glean some basic information from Daphnic, such as evidence of Daphnic's identity and position and qualifications in order to gain a preliminary understanding of his potential value. Central to the matter is what Daphnic is offering at that particular moment, how did he acquire it, and is the information truly credible and useful to the clandestine organization

At some point, the interviewer must make some judgment calls. Is the applicant really who he says he is? Is the information that the applicant offers bona fide? Does he really have access to information of interest? Or is it the sort of thing that an opposing clandestine organization would consider "throw-away" information? Is his stated motivation credible? These judgments can be difficult and often require consultation with others, or a query to the clandestine organization's headquarters. It would be easier if the clandestine operator who receives Daphnic's offer were already acquainted with him, or if it occurs, say, at an event or place where each would normally be present. In such a case, the operator can get back to him at a similar venue. But a cold approach by a volunteer requires a decision whether to meet him again. If so, a follow-up meeting must be discreet, bordering on the clandestine.

If it emerges that the walk-in, Daphnic, is bona fide, and is willing to work on an ongoing basis as a secret agent for the clandestine organization, then (just as in the case of SHARPERSON and HOPEWARS/1) the relationship will require skillful handling, subtlety and tenacity in training Daphnic in the basic principles of operational security and information reporting. If his information is worthwhile, and if it seems that he is in a position to provide continual worthwhile service, and if he is willing to be a secret agent (and not just seeking one-time remuneration, or insisting, perhaps, on defecting immediately), then the clandestine organization will run him as a secret agent.

If that happens, and he is recruited, the task ahead is the same as SHARPERSON's task with the newly-recruited HOPEWARS/1. The task will be to train the new recruit in the basic practices and principles of clandestinity to the point that he is a professional, competent, disciplined, and controlled secret agent. In both cases, the acquisition of the new agent is just the beginning.

Agent Control

Returning to our friend HOPEWARS/1, if he accepts operator SHARPERSON's proposal, he is technically a recruited secret agent from that moment onward. Yet there is much to be done to bring him truly into the fold as a full and trusted secret agent. Many a grizzled old clandestine operator will insist that, in actuality, HOPEWARS/1 cannot be considered "fully recruited" until he has accepted all the control and discipline that a full employer-employee relationship implies.

An important reason for agent control is that a good espionage service cannot make a worth-while contribution solely by reporting tidbits of information from casual sources, snitches, or friendly contacts. The information that a service collects is often of key importance and it <u>must</u> come from trusted and <u>controlled</u> sources. The value of a clandestine service's production is all in the controlled sourcing.

For example, a diplomat from SHARPERSON'S country might hear from a contact that, say, the President of the Republic of Aggressia intends to invade a neighboring country. Since the relationship between the diplomat and the contact is not based on control factors such as salary or emoluments, or on businesslike procedures, it is hard for the diplomat to demand to know all the sourcing and sub-sourcing, to insist on accuracy, or to instruct the contact to seek out more information on one aspect or other.

Of course, the diplomat and the clandestine operator might respectively come up with the same information that Aggressia is planning to attack a neighbor. But the information coming from a controlled agent who will report his sourcing and sub-sourcing in detail is much more valuable than information that is merely elicited. The foregoing is a point that laymen frequently misunderstand. It's all in the sourcing.

HOPEWARS/1's continuing evolution from personal friend who enjoys a profitable discreet relationship with SHARPERSON, to a full, responsive, disciplined, reliable, meticulous, trustworthy secret agent will require skillful handling, subtlety, and tenacity on SHARPERSON's part as their relationship deepens, and as he trains HOPEWARS/1 in his new role as a secret agent.

Almost all recruitments take place in face-to-face meetings between the clandestine operator and the new secret agent. Subsequent face-to-face meetings with a secret agent will follow a definite formal protocol that incorporates all the elements of operational security, as well as the symbiotic interplay between the operator and agent. But meanwhile, SHARPERSON's meetings with HOPEWARS/1 will not be so structured in order not to load too much too quickly onto HOPEWARS/1, which might cause him to have second thoughts about his relationship with SHARPERSON.

CHAPTER III

Face-To-Face Meetings

Personal Meetings

An organization that sponsors clandestine operations generally prefers to communicate with its secret agents regularly and reliably through its clandestine operators. Personal communication is most efficient through face-to-face meetings (although there are impersonal means as well, which we will discuss later.)

<u>The most vulnerable aspect of any clandestine operation involving human beings is the point of contact between the clandestine organization and its secret agents.</u> It is usually done through one of the organization's clandestine operators. The contact must be efficient but it also must be as safe as possible. It is here that the operator must seek the optimal point of efficiency diagrammed in Figure 3 earlier in this book.

And it is also here that the clandestine operator must carefully apply the principles of cover, concealment, and compartmentation. And above all he must train his agent to also understand those principles. The training should usually be a gradual process to ensure that it sinks in well, that the agent not feel undue pressure, and that he remains comfortable in his clandestine role.

All good clandestine operators understand that a fully-recruited, functioning secret agent always has a sense of isolation from the society around him due to the secrecy of his work. It stands to reason that underlying that isolation is an undeniable fear, even if it is suppressed. Any clandestine operator worth his salt will use his face-to-face contact with his agent to convey his sincere interest and understanding of the agent as a person, to reassure him of his personal esteem and concern, and maintain a certain degree of rapport which to begin with was such a big factor in the agent's recruitment.

Cover, Concealment and Compartmentation in Personal Meetings

Cover. No clandestine operator should ever forget **the iron rule that there must be a cover for every clandestine act**. The word "cover" refers to a seemingly legitimate explanation that masks or camouflages clandestinity.

As explained earlier, cover encompasses *status cover*, which explains why a clandestine operator is present in a given country. In the case of SHARPERSON and HOPEWARS/1, their reasons for being in Probahlia are already established; HOPEWARS/1 is a legitimate foreign diplomat, and SHARPERSON most certainly has a legitimate job of some sort. But there is also another type of cover which we call *action cover*, which explains every move they make as part of their clandestine work, and includes an explanation as to why the operator and secret agent are in contact.

A question that a clandestine operator must ask himself is whether the cover explanation for being with an agent would stand up as normal and unsuspicious, and not seem incongruous or likely to be remembered later. There has got to be an ostensible, innocent, and legitimate explanation as to why a clandestine operator meets with an agent. And remember, the explanation must be tailored to the three basic oppositions that exist in a particular operational environment; that is, not only the public opposition, but also law enforcement, and the professional counterintelligence services.

In the case of SHARPERSON and HOPEWARS/1, who are two foreigners in a third country, Probahlia, the sight of them together would not excite the suspicion of the general public, nor of a local policeman, nor is it likely to pique the interest of the local counterintelligence service, provided these contacts are not seen as too frequent or systematic, and that they come across as casual social affairs. So, at this stage of their relationship they are under "social cover" which is probably adequate. Furthermore, they might continue from time to time to have real social contact along with their wives, in order to reinforce the idea that their relationship is indeed strictly a social one, even though now HOPEWARS/1 is a recruited agent. Still, SHARPERSON would want those contacts to become less and less frequent.

Concealment. Indeed, even though the clandestine operator and the secret agent are in Probahlia, a third country, it is still a good idea not to establish too much evidence of frequent contact. So (as mentioned) SHARPERSON and HOPEWARS/1 will meet in different out of the way places so that they will be less likely to be remembered and associated frequently with each other. Such a measure would fall under the rubric of concealment, and would lessen any suspicion or curiosity on the part of the public or local law enforcement, and it would lessen the chance that their contact would come under the suspicion of the professional opposition. Later, in HOPEWARS/1's home country of Degenera, when HOPEWARS/1 is much more liable to be under the normal scrutiny of his superiors and the authorities of his own government, social cover will no longer be sufficient. By then, SHARPERSON hopes that HOPEWARS/1 will have become more accustomed to his role as a secret agent and will accept concealment methods that are more protective (and a better cover story as well).

Compartmentation. SHARPERSON has already emphasized to HOPEWARS/1 that he should keep the fact of their contact as limited as possible even from his wife. But later when greater concealment becomes necessary, they might meet in a house or apartment rented for the clandestine organization by another agent. In such a case the clandestine operator has to consider that compartmentation is somewhat weakened because the other agent knows that the place is used for clandestine meetings with someone else. Also, one has to come up with a cover story as to why they are meeting in such a place.

Follow Up to HOPEWARS/1's Recruitment

A week or so after SHARPERSON's recruitment of HOPEWARS/1, they will meet again. It might be a good idea to schedule the follow-up meetings relatively soon so as best to gauge HOPEWARS/1's state of mind soon after the recruitment.

In line with the imperative that we make a record of all clandestine activities, SHARPERSON will submit an activity report each time he meets with HOPEWARS/1. Of course, each report will note the time, place, and participants, but should mention all security aspects of the meeting, including the cover for the meeting (which would still be "social cover" in the case of SHARPERSON and HOPEWARS/1) and will also mention concealment (perhaps by describing the out-of-the-way location of the meeting site). The report should include a statement of any security anomalies or lack thereof.

Of course, the report should contain a straightforward account of the meeting, and a brief statement of any political information that HOPEWARS/1 may have passed SHARPERSON, which SHARPERSON will report separately in greater detail in an information report (discussed later in this book). The activity report itself should contain any follow up questions or new collection requirements for HOPEWARS/1.

The account of the meeting contained in the activity report should contain a description of HOPEWARS/1's mood, demeanor, and attitude towards his new status as a clandestine reporter, as well as any other aspects that might be useful if someday the clandestine organization decides to make a historical analysis of the exact nature of its relationship with him. (This will be discussed later under the rubric of "counterintelligence.")

Since one of the immediate aspects of the clandestine organization's new secret-agent relationship with HOPEWARS/1 is his growth as a full-fledged trained agent, SHARPERSON will start inculcating some of the basic parameters pertaining to the communication between them. SHARPERSON will carry out such training gradually and informally. This too should be made a matter of record in all activity reports documenting their meetings.

For example, perhaps at this stage SHARPERSON will suggest a separate time and pre-arranged meeting site in case their present meeting is interrupted. Later on, in regular subsequent meetings, SHARPERSON and HOPEWARS/1 will agree on a method to trigger an unscheduled meeting, also at a pre-arranged site. This would occur, for example, if some emergency should arise that they need to discuss, or if HOPEWARS/1 has some new and immediate information to report that cannot wait until the next scheduled meeting. Such arrangements for alternate or unscheduled meetings would require some sort of signal that would obviate the need to make direct contact to set up such a meeting if a situation should warrant it, and it obviously would enhance the security of their relationship. (We will discuss signals later in this book.)

If HOPEWARS/1 is to morph into a full-fledged, disciplined, agent-employee of SHARPERSON's clandestine organization, he will eventually have to work with a different clandestine operator. SHARPERSON will eventually introduce the new operator to HOPEWARS/1, but there might be occasions in which HOPEWARS/1 might have to meet such a person without knowing him or her ahead of time. So SHARPERSON is going to have to set up such a system with HOPEWARS/1, which will also involve signals not only to trigger such a meeting if the time and place is not pre-set, but also to enable the new clandestine operator and the secret agent to confirm to each other that they are who they purport to be.

As SHARPERSON slowly trains HOPEWARS/1 in such procedures, their meetings will begin to take on more and more of a structured format as HOPEWARS/1 settles into a new business-like role as a secret agent. But it is often a good idea not to rush matters with a brand-new agent who might be tempted to back out if it appears that things are more complicated than he had initially bargained for. For the time being, SHARPERSON will keep the meetings relaxed and informal.

Range of Possible Cover Stories

There is no limit to imagination and ingenuity when applying good operational security to a clandestine operator's meetings with a secret agent.

For example, suppose the secret agent is an ill-dressed, ill-educated chambermaid who places listening devices for you in the rooms at a large local hotel, and also keeps track of activities therein. Casual observers among the public might wonder why she is talking so long with a well-dressed foreigner. It would be harder in her case to craft a cover that is self-evident even to members of the public opposition, so she and her clandestine operator should probably rely more on concealment. Perhaps the operator could conceal the <u>fact</u> of their meeting and their <u>identities</u> by renting a room in her hotel while he is ostensibly on a routine business trip. It would allow her to visit the operator easily and unobserved since she works there and has natural access to the inside of the building.

Of course, such an arrangement would offer good concealment, but since every clandestine act requires a cover, she and her clandestine operator would still need a cover story for being in the hotel room together. They might say that the operator, as a guest in the hotel, saw her in the hall as a hotel employee and tipped her to go out and buy something, perhaps a local tourist item or a ticket to a local show, and she is now bringing the item to the operator in his room. In such a case, she should actually go out and procure the item and have it on hand during the meeting. Such a cover for action would protect the significance of the meeting.

If the meeting were to come to the attention of law enforcement or the professional counterintelligence opposition, they might check out the story and perhaps interview the vendor from whom your agent bought the item. The cover story might persuade the law enforcement opposition, but the professional opposition, which knows all about cover stories, might still remain skeptical. However, it is imperative that the clandestine operator and his secret agent stick with the cover story, if only for legal reasons. **Sticking to a cover is another iron rule of clandestinity.**

Conduct of Agent Meetings

As a clandestine operator continuously trains a new agent and accustoms him or her to good security practices, the clandestine operator's conduct of his meetings with his agent should follow a certain pattern, and not be haphazard. It must be efficient and must be attuned to security. And it must complete all items of discussion, because one cannot easily or safely correct any inefficiencies by simply contacting the agent again right afterwards to fill in any gaps.

At the same time, the meeting should not be utterly cold and matter-of-fact. As mentioned earlier in this chapter, the clandestine operator cannot slough off the inevitable pressures, fears and doubts that beset anyone in the role of secret agent. Instead, the operator must be attentive and understanding. No clandestine operator can be successful if he is not attuned and responsive to the emotions of his agents.

That being said, there are three basic themes that should pervade every face-to-face meeting between a clandestine operator and an agent. These are the agent's <u>reporting</u> and the levying of new reporting or action requirements on him; <u>mechanics</u>, such as future and alternate contact and meeting arrangements and security (cover, concealment, and compartmentation); and <u>personal interaction</u>, which would not only reinforce the agent's ties with the clandestine operator, but also allow the operator to stay attuned to the agent's mood and attitude.

The pattern and sequence of an agent meeting can vary with the experience and style of the clandestine operator, but the foregoing commonsensical elements should always be there.

CHAPTER IV

Signals and Counter-Surveillance

Signals are a big deal in clandestine operations. Every clandestine operator must understand the role of signals and the principles behind them. Clandestine operators and secret agents use signals for countless reasons - to schedule a meeting, to alert each other as to their activities. . .and to signal danger!!

But how do we signal danger? It is a very important question that requires elaboration. <u>The short answer is that in most cases, if there is danger one must NOT implement ANY signal.</u>

Consider the following situation. Let's say a secret agent is waiting to meet his clandestine operator at a pre-arranged meeting site but then he suddenly sees a possible danger that should preclude a meeting. Perhaps he spotted surveillance by the professional opposition. Or perhaps he sees someone whom he knows, such as a relative or merely an acquaintance who coincidentally appears and would recognize him and remember him later which would require an explanation as to what he was doing there, or who that fellow was he was talking with, or who was it who picked him up in a car. Or perhaps the agent notices that law enforcement, for some reason or another, is conducting a sweep of the neighborhood and naturally doesn't want either himself or the foreign clandestine operator to be on record as having been in contact.

If there is danger and if you want to abort an operation, or for that matter you are under duress of any kind, or if for any reason a situation suddenly becomes non-conducive for clandestine activity, then the <u>very last thing</u> you want to do is worry about sending any sort of signal, or about deviating from the norm in any way. So then, if one is <u>not</u> to use a danger signal, how does the secret agent signal the clandestine operator not to approach him and to abort the meeting, or let him know that something is wrong?

<u>Good spycraft dictates that the time to execute any signal is when everything is safe; NOT when things are unsafe. If things are NOT safe, then the ABSCENCE of such a safety signal constitutes, itself, a signal of danger.</u> Let us apply this principle to a simple clandestine meeting.

Meeting Signals and Upper Echelon Control

Suppose once again that you, as a clandestine operator, are supposed to make contact with an agent at a specific time, and the agent is waiting for you at a prearranged spot. Let's say the agent believes everything is safe and okay. <u>That</u> is the moment for the agent to display a signal, and the signal that he displays is a <u>safety</u> signal.

The safety signal should be a deviation from the norm, because if it were in conformity with the norm then it wouldn't really be a signal. Furthermore, if everything is safe, there is not much stress in executing such a signal. For example, if the agent normally does <u>not</u> wear sunglasses, he might put on a pair to indicate that everything is safe. If he normally does <u>not</u> display a handkerchief in his breast pocket, he might pull one out to make it visible if he thinks everything is okay. If he usually wears a hat, he might remove it as a safety signal. In short, the signal must be simple. And even though it is a deviation from the norm for the agent, it must not appear out of the ordinary to casual observers, and he should display it only to indicate safety. His safety signal indicates that, from the agent's vantage point, it's okay for the clandestine operator to make contact.

It is important that a safety signal not be a transient gesture such as scratching one's head, or combing one's hair, or wiping one's brow. Such a signal is too easily missed, and requires the clandestine operator to focus continually on his agent rather than taking in the whole environment.

To reiterate the doctrine of signaling either safety and danger, assume the secret agent, for any number of reasons, thinks that there should not be any contact. The way that the secret agent lets the clandestine operator know that he should not make contact is by <u>not</u> executing the safety signal. What he must <u>not</u> do is execute <u>any</u> kind of signal. He should not have to worry about executing a signal at all.

At first blush one would assume that the clandestine operator himself would do the same, and he too would exhibit a safety signal. But that is <u>not</u> so. Why? Because his role is active, but the agent's role is passive. It is the agent who waits for the clandestine operator to approach him, and it is the clandestine operator who actively initiates the contact, so the clandestine operator himself has no need to signal the agent. This principle as to who ultimately decides to make the contact is known as "upper-echelon control."

Why is it the clandestine operator's decision as to whether to make the approach? Because the clandestine operator is the professional who is in closer touch with his sponsoring organization and also has available to him information from other sources. He is more up-to-date on the latest security information. And he is better trained in operational security. Upper-echelon control dictates that in normal face-to-face clandestine contacts, it is the higher level present that makes the final decision. But there can be exceptions to this rule in cases involving more than simple face-to-face contact.

For example, when the agent goes to an apartment to meet a clandestine operator who is in the apartment waiting there for him, it is the operator, not the agent, who displays the safety signal. It might be a folded newspaper outside the front door, the absence of which would tell the agent not to knock and seek admittance. (A location of this type is known as a "safehouse" and will be discussed later.)

Or in sending a secret message either to or from a clandestine operator, it is the sender who should include in the text a pre-arranged word or phrase that seems natural and unsuspicious to indicate that the message is bona fide and is not sent under duress. One should not have to strive to include a previously-arranged word as a danger signal if one has a gun pointed at one's head. In such a case, you merely omit the word or phrase, and that omission is in itself a danger signal. In all cases, it is the <u>absence</u> of a safety signal that signals danger.

Regardless of the particular situation and regardless of who does the signaling, it remains a basic principle of spycraft not to execute danger signals, but instead to rely on safety signals and, if there is danger, to rely on the absence thereof as an indicator of danger.

I remember a case in which a school was located in a volatile area that was subject to terrorist incursions. The school authorities mandated that if the school were in danger, a certain physical signal - a flag visible at a distance - should be displayed to warn the school bus driver to turn around and not bring the children to the school that morning. The foregoing is precisely what should have <u>not</u> be done. When under stress you don't want to have the added chore of having to raise a signal. Instead, the flag should have been displayed <u>only</u> when the situation was safe; not when it was dangerous. Better than a flag, which an enemy who had previously cased the site might realize was a signal, perhaps something less signal-like would be preferable, such as a large potted plant wheeled out onto the balcony when things were safe, or closing the shades in an upper window in safe situations.

Other Signals

In clandestine operations, one does not use signals just to indicate safe conditions, but also to trigger non-scheduled emergency meetings, or to confirm one's bona fides to another person when there is to be contact between previously unknown people, or to recontact a previous agent, or to signal safety in non-personal communication (such as a letter, as mentioned above, or other techniques which we will elaborate in a later chapter).

We have already discussed the need for a secret agent to display a safety signal to his clandestine operator before the latter will approach to make contact. If for some reason the agent doesn't give the signal, the meeting will be aborted and each will go his separate way without linking up, and they will instead implement their pre-arranged alternate meeting arrangements later. Of course, at the alternate meeting, a safety signal should also play a part.

If either the agent or the clandestine operator wants to arrange an unscheduled meeting due to some urgency, then there must be a signal by which either of them can trigger such a meeting. For example, it might be a telephone call from a public telephone, and the caller would use a coded phrase (which would not only identify him but serve as a safety signal) that would trigger a meeting which would be at a pre-arranged site not mentioned on the telephone. The time might also be prearranged, such as noon the next day. But if not prearranged it can also be worked out in the telephone conversation. In such a case it is important not to mention the actual time over the telephone. Instead let it be in accordance with a pre-arranged formula, say one day and five hours earlier than the one given on the telephone. For example, one can call the other from a public phone and say, "This is Ruabi, and I would like to meet with Hassan (fictitious names) at the rug bazaar at 5:00 PM the day after tomorrow." Whereupon the recipient of the call will say "You have the wrong number, there is nobody named Hassan here," and hang up. But now he knows he is actually to meet the other person tomorrow at noon (one day and five hours earlier than actually said) at a certain café out of town.

There is no limit to the kind of signal one may devise to trigger an unscheduled meeting. If not a telephone call, it might be a physical signal such as a mark on a wall which the agent and the clandestine operator pass each day on the way to work. Or it might be a specific printed commercial brochure that one mails to the other, triggering a meeting the following day or a few days later at a preset hour and place. Or it can be a notice in the "personals" section of the daily newspaper. Or the clandestine operator might place some decoration in the window of his apartment, assuming the agent passes by his building every day and can see it. The agent can have a different signal of his own for his clandestine operator.

If a meeting is between two people who are not previously known to each other, the agent must display, in addition to a pre-arranged safety signal, some sort of physical recognition signal. It might be a distinctive hat, or briefcase, or necktie, or else a shopping bag from a well-known store. The clandestine operator, who is the upper echelon, would not display any physical recognition signal at all in such cases because he might for some reason decide not to make contact and does not want the agent to know who he is and be able to describe him. But if the clandestine operator does decide to make contact, he might approach the agent and say for example, "Do you know if there is a hardware store near here," which would constitute a verbal recognition signal. The agent might reply "Most stores around here are not well stocked," and thus they will confirm themselves definitively to each other.

If perhaps after a long hiatus there is no pre-arranged contact scheduled, or if the sponsoring service wants to re-establish contact with a former agent, the former agent might have been instructed to accept as bona fide anyone who approaches him <u>at any time or at any place</u>, and, again as an example, says to him, "Astrologers say this is a lucky day for optimists," and the agent would then respond, "But what do astronomers say?" In this way both participants will establish their bona fides and can either hold a meeting or set up a meeting to take place later.

Sometimes (usually in Hollywood movies) bona fides are established with physical objects. For example, the clandestine operator displays a distinctive key chain, and the agent produces a distinctive pocket watch. Or sometimes each has a torn half of a photo or a banknote, which fit when put together. The difficulty with this system is that often the distinctive object is lost or mislaid, leaving it impossible to confirm bona fides later.

Counter-surveillance

A seasoned agent who is ready for contact with his clandestine operator will not only give a safety signal if he thinks contact is safe, but will have taken pains earlier to ensure that he has not been deliberately followed. Ditto, the clandestine operator will also check to ensure that he himself is not under surveillance.

Many people often suspect they are under surveillance when in actuality they are not. I have seen this suspicion in all sorts of people; sometimes in successful people who need to believe they are important enough for a security service or other organization to devote much manpower and funds to surveil them. I have seen it in people who feel inordinate guilt for things they have done; perhaps a theft, perhaps an infidelity, or some other deed. But, yes, occasionally they might really be under surveillance.

There is no way to tell for certain that someone is _not_ under surveillance, but there _is_ a methodology for determining with a high degree of accuracy if one _is_. Every clandestine operator, and every fully-recruited secret agent must understand the methodology well.

The method requires the application of three criteria: 1) time, 2) location, and 3) direction. One might notice the same person or people more than once during one's daily movements, but this can be a mere coincidence if they are always moving in the same direction, or if it is around the same time every day, or if it's in the same general locality. In such cases both may have regular legitimate business that coincidentally brings them together. <u>But,</u> if one sees the same person (or persons) at three different times, when one is going first in one direction, then later in another direction, and then even later going in yet a third direction, then one must assume that the "coincidence" is simply too great and that one is under surveillance.

In order to implement the foregoing principle, it is necessary to plan a counter-surveillance route that enables the secret agent or the clandestine operator to go to different places at different times and be moving in a different direction each time. Furthermore, each place must afford an opportunity for him to check who might be behind him without appearing to do so.

One must remember a key point: Innocent people don't normally check for surveillance. A surveillant who sees his target checking for surveillance knows immediately that his target is "tail conscious" and is engaging in something clandestine. Why? Because <u>counter-surveillance is in itself a clandestine act</u>. Therefore, one must mask counter-surveillance by means of cover and concealment.

The cover that one employs for checking for surveillance, and the concealment one employs when making one's observations, must readily appear as innocent acts to the casual observer as well as to any law enforcement personnel who might see you, and also to any surveillants of the professional opposition. One simply cannot go out and wander aimlessly for no apparent reason to check for surveillance because that is a tip-off as to what you are doing. And, of course, one must not appear to be looking purposefully around or behind one's self.

Example of a Simple Counter-Surveillance Route

Below (and in Figure 6) is a typical example of a very simple and very basic counter-surveillance route that you might take prior to a clandestine meeting to make sure you aren't under surveillance:

<u>First</u>, you might emerge from your apartment building and, as cover for action, have a bag of dirty clothes which you carry while walking west to a public laundry. Once inside the relatively dark establishment, you could look back out of the window and take note of anybody on the street behind you. Thanks to the low light inside, you can easily conceal your observation from anybody outside You would then leave your dirty laundry and go out again.

<u>Second</u>, you might then emerge and walk south to a bookstore. Once inside, you could again look discreetly out to the street and note anybody behind you, and then buy a book or magazine as cover for having gone in.

<u>Third</u>, once more out on the street, you could walk east to a café which you would enter and once again look out from inside to see who was behind you. Then you can have a coffee and pastry as cover for going into the café.

SIMPLE FOOT COUNTER-SURVEILLANCE ROUTE

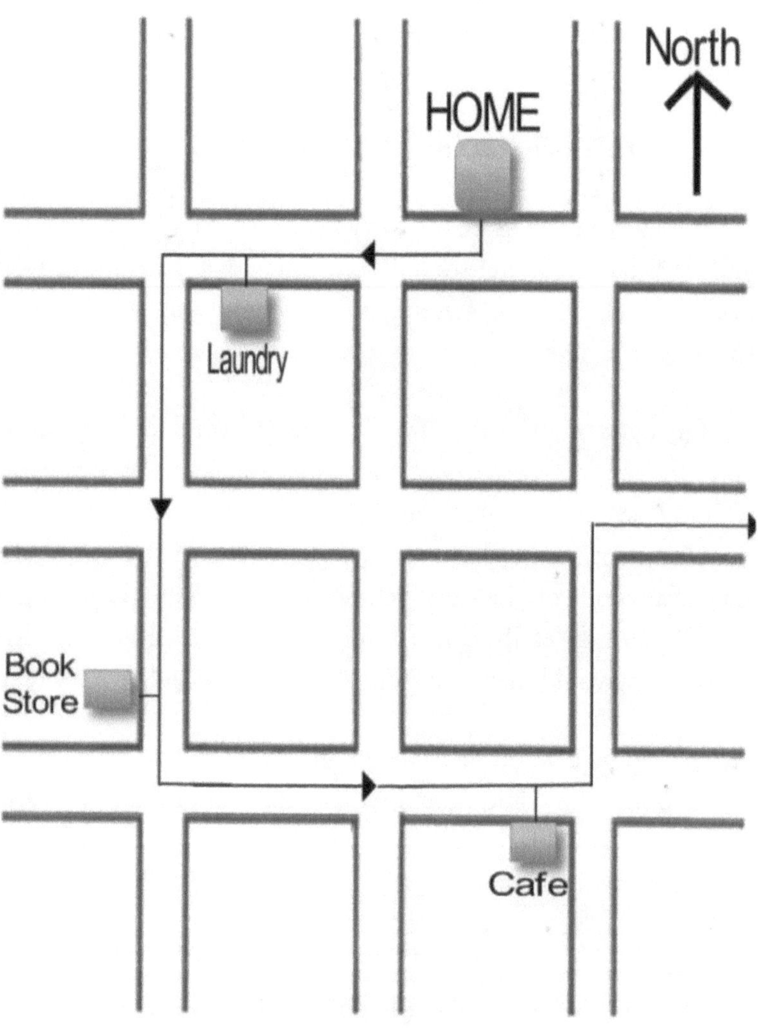

Figure 6

One of the benefits of this system is that at each stop, your surveillance has to stop too. At least one of the surveillants has to monitor the establishment so he can signal to his colleagues to resume the moving surveillance once the target goes out again. Surveillance teams hate such stops because it renders them immobile and makes them more vulnerable to detection. They have to hang around, usually with no apparent cover for doing so, and often with little concealment. Remember that they too are engaging in clandestine activity and they too require cover and concealment for protection. When you choose a counter-surveillance route, a desirable factor would be the lack of opportunity for any surveillant to use concealment or cover.

After a minimum of three such checks for surveillance, you would make your decision. If you had seen at least one same person from all three of your observation points you would assume that it was a surveillant. It would simply be too much of a coincidence that the same person would be behind you at three different times, at three different places, and always going in the same direction that you were going. If you spotted no surveillance, you could proceed to your clandestine contact with some assurance that you were "clean" of surveillance. If not, you should abort the clandestine activity that you had planned.

If you have to abort your planned clandestine activity and instead return home after walking the counter-surveillance route, you would hope that the opposition's surveillance-team report would be a humdrum description of an hour's morning outing with nothing unusual noted and, after a number of such dull events, convince the professional opposition to diminish its scrutiny of your activities, being convinced that you are probably on the up and up, and not to waste further expensive manpower tailing you.

There are also more elaborate and sophisticated methods of detecting surveillance. For example, one might have a colleague stationed in concealed places along the counter-surveillance route, moving from one concealed place to another, to observe you when you are at different places and going in different directions at different times. He would then give you an "all clear" safety signal at the end if indeed he detects no surveillance. In some cities a person in a high-rise building might get a very clear view of the layout behind you. Or else, you can have your own friendly surveillance team follow you, and they might detect any hostile surveillance against you by someone else, and then signal you accordingly.

Nevertheless, the foregoing methods consume resources and are often simply not practical, and not necessary in most operating climates. However if the operating climate is very difficult, it is usually the better part of wisdom for a clandestine operator to minimize his clandestine activities drastically. In such a climate, it is far more likely the clandestine operator would be under scrutiny as a foreigner in the country. The big fear of any clandestine operation is that if the clandestine operator is under surveillance, he might lead the professional opposition right to his secret agent.

The secret agent himself, who is perhaps an information source who is a member of the local culture and has a legitimate position as a penetration of a target, is probably less likely to be initially suspect. Still he must engage in counter-surveillance just in case, and he must abort any contact if he believes he is being watched.

It should be obvious that when operating in a very hostile atmosphere, most intelligence operators prefer to rely on impersonal methods of communication that don't require direct contact. (Such methods will be discussed later.) In these cases, direct contact is used very sparingly. Or else the clandestine operator would limit direct contact to times when the secret agent is traveling outside his country.

A word about vehicles is in order. There is considerable doctrine as to vehicular counter-surveillance. One might, for example, take a number of turns and check in one's rear view mirror to see the vehicles that are behind, but there must be a cover for making those turns. Being inside a car with a rear-view mirror affords adequate concealment for looking behind, but one still needs a self-evident cover for the route one is taking. As in foot counter-surveillance, one should choose a relatively unfrequented route, and preferably a route that requires turns and changes of direction in order to get to a given destination. Obviously, routes that are nearly deserted are preferable provided there is a good cover for taking them, such as a reasonable way to get to a given restaurant, park, hotel or similar venue.

Regardless of the degree of sophistication of a counter-surveillance technique, whether vehicular or on foot, the governing principle is that it must encompasses at least three different checkpoints for observing possible surveillance at three different times while moving successively in a different direction at each of three different places.

Another governing principle is that the operator should try to avoid impromptu counter-surveillance. Instead the operator must meticulously plan counter-surveillance routes ahead of time. Do not try to be clever like some cool spy in the movies who "thinks on his feet," and who tries some impromptu maneuver to spot or evade surveillance. If the opposition judges that you are trying to detect or evade surveillance, you have then given yourself away and your usefulness is at an end. Never underestimate the professional opposition. Never think that your *ad hoc*, quick knee-jerk common sense will trump the careful scrutiny of experienced professionals.

Surveillance Itself

Every clandestine operator should know how to conduct moving surveillance of a target; for there is no better way to sensitize the operator to the concerns, techniques and mannerisms of those who may in turn be performing surveillance on him. Furthermore, as a clandestine operator in a foreign country, he may have to recruit and build his own surveillance capability composed of local agents.

We should understand that no clandestine organization operating outside its own country carries out surveillance without careful consideration of its potential value and risks. A clandestine organization operating abroad would not have sufficient control of the environment, nor the resources to mount an expensive and time-consuming moving surveillance of an individual if the risks of compromise were too great. Accordingly, surveillance would probably be against such unsuspecting individuals as recruitment targets who have no inkling that they might be objects of scrutiny, and about whom we would be seeking background information as to, say, susceptibilities, vulnerabilities, activities, interests and contacts. But one is normally less likely to mount such moving surveillance against a suspected hostile operator trained in counter-surveillance tactics lest the hostile operator detect the surveillance, put himself on guard, and compromise the surveillants. Or else such surveillance in a foreign country might be of the static type, such as casing a target-building for a possible surreptitious entry or for possible use as a safehouse.

On the other hand, a counterintelligence service operating with legal authority in its own country, and in control of the environment, usually has more resources and personnel, and might be more willing to target a suspected foreign clandestine operator or a local person suspected of being an agent of a foreign clandestine service. Such a counterintelligence service knows all about counter-surveillance techniques that a target might use, and would be able to produce a large contingent of surveillants experienced in shifting positions and cleverly changing places with each other and enjoying sophisticated means of communication among themselves. In return, the clandestine operator who is their target might employ more and more sophisticated counter-surveillance techniques, such as (already mentioned) having one or more confederates stationed in concealed places along the counter-surveillance route who would coordinate and communicate among themselves and then signal to him whether he was "clean" or not.

But except in very exigent circumstances, it is unlikely that a foreign clandestine organization operating abroad in an increasingly hostile operating environment would want to engage in such elaborate counter-surveillance activities. Instead it might want to minimize the danger of face-to-face meetings, and rely on non-personal means of communication with its agents. We will discuss these in a later chapter. In such a case, face-to-face meetings would be infrequent and perhaps take place only when the agent is travelling abroad.

There is always the danger of scrutiny by a hostile professional opposition, which is why counter-surveillance is a must. This is true even in a relatively safe environment, even where one doubts that he has come under scrutiny, even when face-to-face meetings are feasible and the operator and agent have excellent cover for meeting with each other. The operating environment can easily change, and if one has already come under suspicion of the local professional counterintelligence opposition, the latter would not be likely to swallow a cover story. So, if counterintelligence efforts should indicate any unwelcome scrutiny, the operator should abort the meeting; and if the agent detects the same, he must not display a safety signal. In such cases, the clandestine service, the operator, and the agent, must re-think their means of communication.

Surveillance Tactics

Note that an experienced surveillance team, comprising more than just three people and accustomed to working together, usually develops its own protocols to follow a target, shift positions, and thereby minimize the chance that a target will detect them. It is beyond the scope of this book to delve into the complex mechanics of surveillance, but we can explain in a simple way how a small three-man team might shift positions when a target, say, turns a corner. Even this simple tactic is somewhat complicated, but the reader who will take a minute to focus on it will find it revealing. (See Figure 7.)

It starts with target X walking east. Behind him at a discreet distance is the lead surveillant A, and behind lead surveillant A at yet another further discreet distance is a second surveillant B. Meanwhile, across the street is a third surveillant C.

If X turns right at a cross street and starts walking south, surveillant A does <u>not</u> turn right to stay behind him. Instead he crosses the cross street and starts walking south, so he now takes the same position across the street from X and relative to X that C had when they were moving east.

Meanwhile, surveillant B turns right and stays behind X and now becomes the lead surveillant, while C crosses the original street they were on and now moves south as the second surveillant behind the new lead surveillant B, thereby assuming the position that B had before when they were all moving east. In this manner, the "people landscape" behind target X changes.

Sound complicated? For surveillance teams that work together a lot, such maneuvers become second nature and can be particularly deceptive to a surveillance target, especially if the surveillance team consists of more than three people who shift positions in different ways.

Further Post-Recruitment Development of HOPEWARS/1

At the moment, HOPEWARS/1 probably still sees himself as merely a personal friend who is helping SHARPERSON while at the same time profiting from SHARPERSON's access to funds. Even though HOPEWARS/1 will remain in Probahlia for a full year before he returns to Degenera, it might be too much to expect that during that year HOPEWARS/1 would accept the full paraphernalia of spycraft practices and principles in what is still a personal relationship.

SIMPLE SURVEILLANCE TEAM POSITION CHANGE

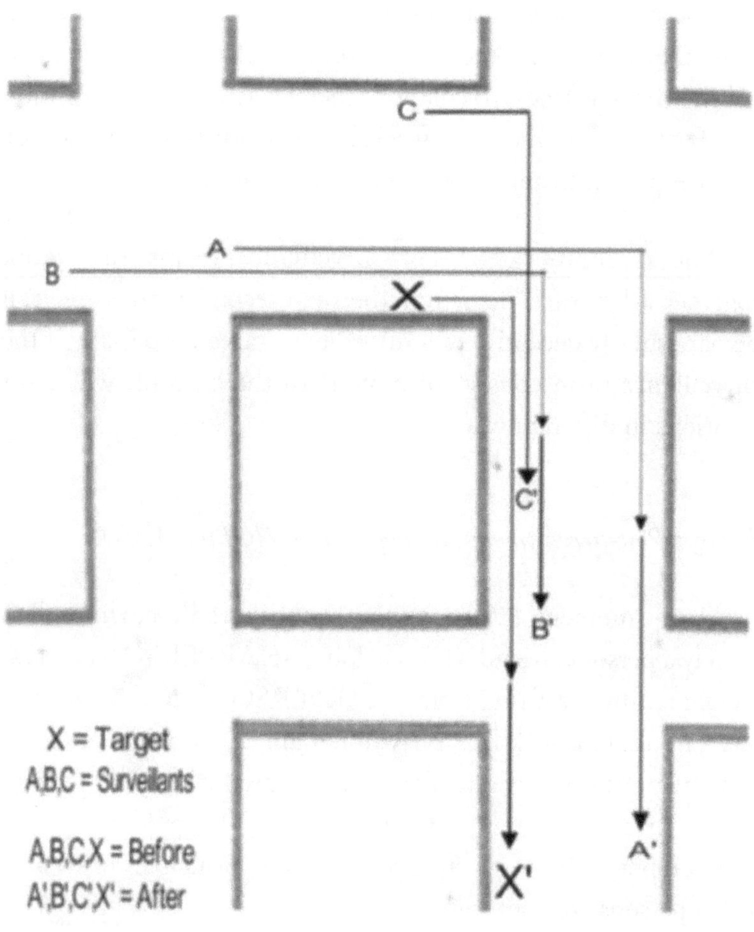

Figure 7

Nevertheless, SHARPERSON will gently try to inculcate and reinforce the idea that HOPEWARS/1 should go to their contact point by means of a route that is not too heavily traveled to make sure that nobody is following him. On top of this, they will always select their next time and place of contact while at a regular meeting, and have a provision for an alternate meeting in case they are interrupted or if, for one reason or another, one of the two parties does not show up.

In the case of HOPEWARS/1, even the use of safety signals prior to any face-to-face contact, or even a secret signal to trigger an unscheduled meeting, would be suggestive to him of true spying that would be far and above the simple passage of information in the context of a friendship between two foreigners in a third country. Ditto for training in counter-surveillance or otherwise imposing more of the panoply of operational security on HOPEWARS/1. So SHARPERSON will work on making HOPEWARS/1 feel fully comfortable in his role as a discreet informant, and hope he becomes dependent on his monthly payments before assuming that HOPEWARS/1 is ready to accept his full secret role. It might be necessary to wait until HOPEWARS/1 is about to return to Degenera, where he realizes that his activities might be more dangerous and must truly be kept secret, especially if he is by then reporting significantly on his own country.

Such continued development of an agent, especially in the period immediately following his recruitment, can be very dicey since there is always the possibility that he will suddenly rethink his commitment and change his mind. There is a perception among old clandestine operators that a recruited agent isn't truly an agent until a year or so after his recruitment.

Preparing HOPEWARS/1 for his Return to his Home Country

During their remaining year together, SHARPERSON will also convey to HOPEWARS/1 the basic principles of information reporting (discussed in a later chapter), and gradually start emphasizing SHARPERSON's interest in Degeneran affairs in the hope that HOPEWARS/1 will feel more and more willing to report on his own country. SHARPERSON will also continue his financial generosity, not only paying HOPEWARS/1 the agreed-on monthly stipend of $1,000, but giving him frequent bonuses for exceptionally good information.

But finally, HOPEWARS/1's tour of duty in Probahlia will come to an end, and his return to Degenera will be imminent. Now comes The Great Moment of Truth. Will HOPEWARS/1 be willing to continue a discreet relationship with SHARPERSON or one of SHARPERSON's colleagues in Degenera, and will he be willing to report on his own country?

SHARPERSON will now perhaps break from what has become a normally discreet contact with HOPEWARS/1, and return briefly to their social relationship by setting up dinner at SHARPERSON's home where HOPEWARS/1 can meet an old friend of SHARPERSON's who is visiting Probahlia but who may soon be living and working in Degenera, and who is eager to meet a Degeneran.

At their evening together, SHARPERSON's friend, who is really HANDLEMAN, a skilled clandestine operator who is fully briefed on HOPEWARS/1's character, personality, background, and interests, hits it off well with HOPEWARS/1. They part with mutual expressions of how delightful it was to have met and that they each hope that they might someday meet again.

Eventually, in asking HOPEWARS/1 to continue his relationship back in Degenera with SHARPERSON's organization, SHARPERSON might suggest that HANDLEMAN be the contact, and ask HOPEWARS/1's permission to brief HANDLEMAN on their relationship. If HOPEWARS/1 demurs, the contact with SHARPERSON can still continue with frequent visits by SHARPERSON to Degenera, or during HOPEWARS/1's travels outside of Degenera (undertaken with good cover). On the other hand, if HOPEWARS/1 says okay to maintaining contact with HANDLEMAN inside Degenera, they can then set up the parameters of such a contact, perhaps during another visit by HANDLEMAN to Probahlia.

If the foregoing unfolds well, and if HOPEWARS/1 agrees to discreet contact with HANDLEMAN in Degenera, it will constitute a major achievement. SHARPERSON's clandestine organization would now be one step closer to having a secret penetration of the Degeneran Air Force at the headquarters level. In the case of HOPEWARS/1, both Probahlia and Degenera are legitimate targets. HOPEWARS/1 has been helpful with regard to Probahlia and has given some indication of his willingness while in Probahlia to report on Degeneran matters but, with regard to the latter, the commitment is not yet spelled out, and clandestine operator SHARPERSON must proceed with care to do it before HOPEWARS/1 goes home.

However, there is every reason for SHARPERSON and HANDLEMAN to feel optimistic that HOPEWARS/1 will be willing to report on Degeneran matters which he has already done occasionally with SHARPERSON in the past. Such a willingness is now deeply implied if HOPEWARS/1 acquiesces to meeting HANDLEMAN in Degenera itself. The parameters for contact in Degenera will no longer have a semi-overt component as it did in

Probahlia where it was based on HOPEWARS/1's original social relationship with SHARPERSON. Instead it will be utterly secret, and more carefully concealed. It is likely that HANDLEMAN and HOPEWARS/1 will meet in a safehouse (see next chapter).

Comment on Time and Patience

The long interpersonal development with HOPEWARS/1 (a couple of years) during which SHARPERSON skillfully orchestrated the latter's recruitment, and the additional year of development afterward, indicates how time consuming the acquisition of agents can be. It further illustrates the patience and time necessary to properly consummate such an agent-acquisition operation.

That is why many countries will engage in recruitment operations against other countries that are not inimical to them, and against whom the acquisition of clandestine sources might not be a priority. History shows that except in the case of the most stable allies, a country can turn from friendly to unfriendly in the twinkle of an eye. If at such a time the sponsoring organization does not have agents in that country, or is unable to conjure up immediately a set of well-placed agents, it is subject to criticism from the customer for "a failure of intelligence." So, it is incumbent on sponsoring clandestine organizations to insist vigorously on adequate budgets from their customers in order to support clandestine activities, even if it would seem "unnecessary" in a given place at a given moment. The customers of a clandestine organization must grasp that, ultimately, there are few genuine friendships among sovereign nations.

CHAPTER V

Safehouses

Safehouses, as mentioned earlier, are houses or apartments that are under the covert control of the sponsoring clandestine organization and which offer safety and concealment for clandestine activities. Normally there should be no visible connection between the sponsoring clandestine organization and the person who owns or rents a safehouse, not only for the sake of deniability but to minimize any curiosity by the local opposition as to a possible illegal connection.

An important caveat must be attached to safehouses. Despite their great value in concealing clandestine contacts and activities, one can never say that a safehouse is completely safe. The major security threat of a safehouse lies in weakened compartmentation. In a foreign country, it is a local agent who usually owns or rents a safehouse, has a legitimate reason for it, and is the "safehouse keeper." He then allows a clandestine operator to use it as the operator sees fit. But the fact remains that the safehouse keeper himself is aware that someone is using the premises for clandestine purposes which adds a vulnerability to the arrangement in the form of broken compartmentation. Still, many clandestine operators believe that the security advantages of a properly-used safehouse vastly outweigh its dangers.

In the context of "properly-used," a clandestine operator should observe all the basic tools of clandestinity when using a safehouse. For example, so as not to further erode compartmentation, a clandestine operator should never use a safehouse for more than one agent lest a compromise of the one agent lead to the compromise of others. Furthermore, there should always be a cover story as to why someone is in the safehouse and why he is meeting someone there.

And, of course, to increase concealment, one must check for surveillance and be reasonably certain one is not followed or observed when going to the safehouse. Last, as mentioned earlier, there must be a safety signal that conveys to the secret agent that it is safe to seek entrance. <u>Here one can ignore the "upper echelon control" rule (previous chapter). The person waiting in the safehouse initiates the signal, whether it be the clandestine operator or the agent.</u>

Examples of Safehouses

Safehouses as concealment for clandestine activity have an ancient history. The earliest known safehouse keeper (mentioned in the Old Testament) was a prostitute named Rahab who owned an apartment in Jericho that was built into the walls of the city. She made it available to Joshua's men when they came secretly to case ("spy out") Jericho prior to putting it under siege circa 1500-1400 BC. There is no record in the Bible of any cover story for its use if they had been discovered there (although given her profession, it must have been obvious), but there is a record of a recognition signal that Rahab displayed at the premises so that Joshua's troops would not destroy it after the conquest of the town.

Another example is in the New Testament. When Jesus and his followers came to Jerusalem around 30 AD to foment what was eventually an unsuccessful insurrection, Jesus needed a place to meet his key people and plan their next move. He sent two of his clandestine operators into the city to contact an agent of their movement who would be carrying a pitcher of water as a recognition signal. The agent led them to a safehouse where they would later gather together. The cover story for the gathering would be, of course, the celebration of the Passover meal.

In my earlier book, *My CIA: Memories of a Secret Career*, I gave an example of a safehouse I once used to meet a particularly attractive female agent who was a public figure in the country where I was operating. It was absolutely necessary that we meet in concealed conditions to avoid the risk of someone recognizing her when she was with me. In this case I rented the safehouse myself, ostensibly as a retreat for writing a tourist handbook, and I stocked it with notes, photos, reference material, and a typewriter. While my direct rental of the safehouse avoided the compartmentation problem inherent in a separate safehouse keeper, it did link the safehouse to someone of my nationality. But I thought the risk was minimal in that environment which was not particularly hostile, and where such rentals are informal affairs.

I will add here that the safehouse was in an anonymous albeit somewhat small apartment building with no attendant who might remember anyone's comings and goings. As a safety signal I would leave an advertising brochure stuck in the door handle. If we were ever discovered together, the true significance of our meeting would be disguised by the cover story that we were lovers. We even concocted a history of how we had met and fallen in love. I used this apartment with this agent only.

A room in a large anonymous hotel can also serve as a safehouse, albeit a temporary one. Say the clandestine operator lives in an outer suburb of Merzulia, the capital city of Degenera. Once a month he and his wife go into downtown Metzulia for a night on the town and they would rent a room in a large hotel for the night so he wouldn't have to drive home tired and with any drinks in him. This would offer an ideal opportunity for the operator to meet with an agent. The agent could go to the hotel and, if it is a large and anonymous one, go to the operator's room. Or the agent might also get a room himself under a suitable pretext which would make it even easier to get inside the building and then go to the operator's room. In this case there must also be a cover story in case they have to explain why they're in a room together.

The hotel room scenario might also work as a concealed meeting venue for HANDLEMAN and HOPEWARS/1. However, if HANDLEMAN ever comes under the suspicion of the professional opposition, one can be sure that the professionals will check the list of all guests who are present in the hotel whenever HANDLEMAN is there. They will notice HOPEWARS/1's presence in the hotel at every such time, and they would know that it would be too much of a coincidence. Furthermore, even if HOPEWARS/1 does not rent a room for himself, the professional opposition might check the comings and goings at the hotel if HANDLEMAN is ever under suspicion. This would be true in a particularly harsh operating environment. Also, such a hotel room fails to disguise the link between the renter and the clandestine operator's country, so another safehouse with no foreign ties would be better. This is a matter for the clandestine operator's judgment. (Figure 8).

Although there is great advantage to using a non-hotel safehouse as a concealment tool, we again emphasize that there is a weakening of compartmentation if one uses a local agent to buy or rent it. But many a clandestine operator would accept the slight risk to compartmentation even if the cover story for using it were a little lame. Such a course would probably not be acceptable in a very hostile operating environment with a near-totalitarian professional opposition. In such cases, communication with the agent would probably be through non-personal means (described in a later chapter), or by using a clandestine operator who himself is an experienced agent and also a citizen of the country where he is operating, and therefore less likely to trigger the scrutiny of the professional opposition. Or else, contacts would be through meetings that would take place during visits to some other country.

Although Degenera is an authoritarian state that is not on the friendliest terms with HANDLEMAN's country, it does not have the manpower nor the desire to place all foreigners under intense scrutiny, nor has it reached the totalitarian level that would make anyone's contact with a foreigner dangerous. While HANDLEMAN could therefore probably meet safely with HOPEWARS/1 at varying out-of-the way public locations, he is still not keen on doing it, especially if HOPEWARS/1 ends up in a sensitive position within his own government. On balance, HANDLEMAN decides to use a safehouse for his regularly-scheduled contacts with HOPEWARS/1. Also, HOPEWARS/1, might feel more secure meeting HANDLEMAN under concealment, it being less likely to evoke questions than if he met him in public.

DECISION TO ACQUIRE A SAFEHOUSE

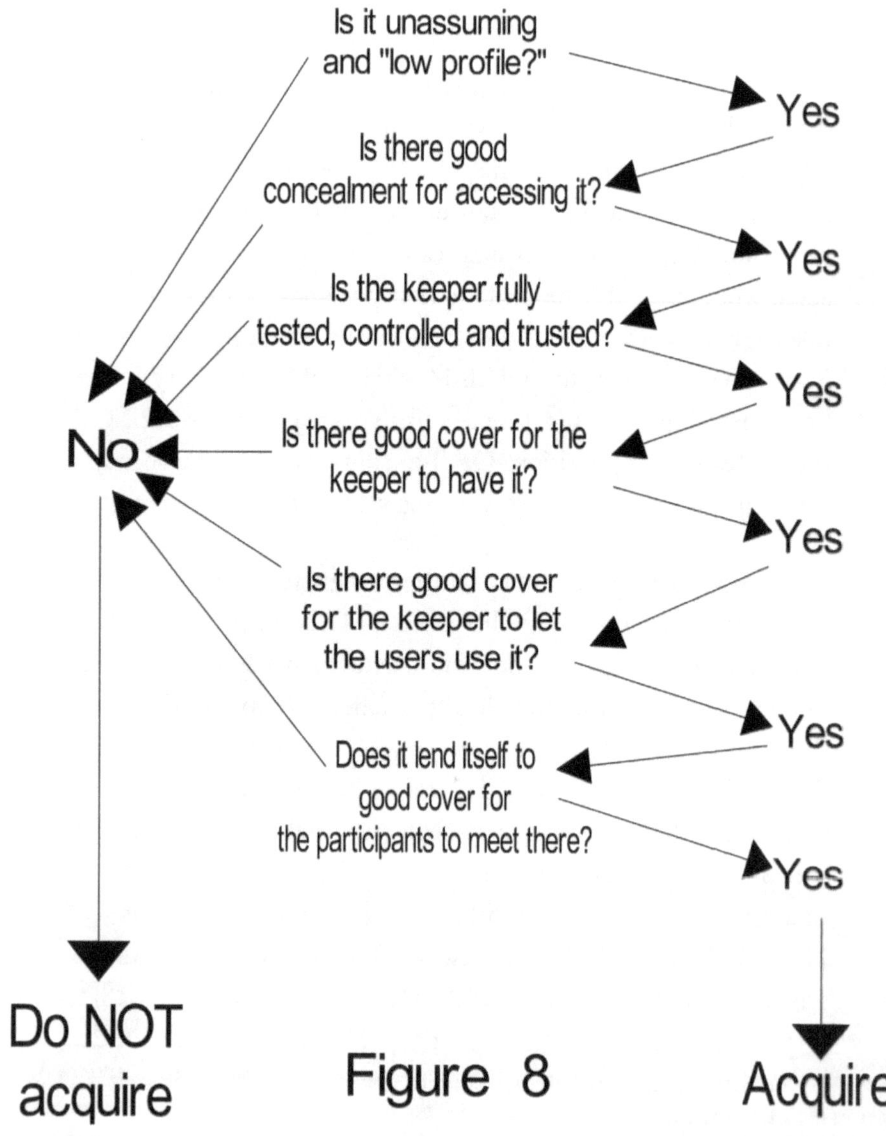

Figure 8

A Safehouse for HOPEWARS/1

An almost ideal arrangement that would cover, conceal, and compartment any contact between HANDLEMAN and HOPEWARS/1 would be if both HANDLEMAN and his wife were to live in the same large apartment building as HOPEWARS/1 and his wife. In such a case, HANDLEMAN's own apartment would be an almost perfect safehouse, due to proximity and concealment.

Under near-perfect concealment, HOPEWARS/1 could leave his apartment and go (perhaps by way of a stairwell if on a different floor in order to minimize accidental contacts on the way) to HANDLEMAN's apartment for a relaxed undisturbed meeting. He would, of course, have a cover story for his absence from his own apartment. If, however, the actual contact with HANDLEMAN were discovered, it would probably suffice to invoke social cover of two friendly neighbors simply having a drink together; both would have a cover story of how they originally met in the building, became acquainted, share common interests, and so forth.

However, a true safehouse is best untainted by any connection to the sponsoring organization's home country. For this reason, if a clandestine operator uses his own home or a place that he rents himself, it precludes deniability in terms of the operator's country, and it could also be subject to routine scrutiny because of its foreign connection. It might be subject to wiretaps, microphones, and so forth. Again, such a disadvantage depends on the operating environment and the degree of control the government has over its society. Still, the advantages of such a setup in terms of cover, concealment, and compartmentation might dwarf the disadvantages, or it might not.

Another problem is that it is unlikely that such an ideal setup can be found, and it might be incongruous financially for HOPEWARS/1 to afford an apartment in the same building as HANDLEMAN's without assuming some improper source of funds. So, after much thought, HANDLEMAN's clandestine office in Degenera decides that a separate safehouse, controlled by a local and well-trusted agent, would be the best bet.

Such a local and well-trusted agent is HOMEMAKER/3, a Degeneran agent run by HANDLEMAN's sponsoring clandestine organization. She is an expensive call girl who can plausibly maintain an apartment to entertain her clients. HANDLEMAN's office has now asked her to acquire such an apartment ostensibly for her own professional use.

HOMEMAKER/3 is what is known as a support agent. She does not report political or economic information, but performs chores in support of her sponsor's clandestine operations. Her profession allows her to go to most parts of town including the less reputable neighborhoods. She can surveil people, observe buildings and establishments of interest, or retrieve material hidden by other agents for passage to her sponsoring organization. (More on non-personal communication in a later chapter.)

Over the years, she has saved most of her remuneration from the clandestine organization. She keeps the bulk of it in an interest-bearing bank fund in a third country where her finances would not likely be under scrutiny by her government. The fact that she saves much of her clandestine remuneration has precluded her from attracting too much current attention due to an excess of wealth, and she can convincingly live a somewhat comfortable life-style ostensibly from her success in her profession. Furthermore, if she were to come under the scrutiny of the local authorities, either by law enforcement or professional counterintelligence personnel, it would be perfectly natural for someone in her profession not to keep records of her activities, and for her contacts and assets to be unnamed and difficult to trace. Last, her reliability and honesty on behalf of HANDLEMAN's organization has been tested over the years.

For the time being, in keeping with good security practices, HOMEMAKER/3's safehouse will be used solely for the HOPEWARS/I operation. HOMEMAKER/3's apartment is not going to be in an upscale part of town. She will rent it on a month-to-month basis with no lease or paper trail, a not uncommon practice in many countries like Degenera. The owner from whom HOMEMAKER/3 rents the apartment might not even know HOMEMAKER/3's name, or she might use a false name, no questions asked. She will decorate it and stock it with things that indicate that it is a woman's home.

HANDLEMAN and HOPEWARS/1 will each check for surveillance before going to the safehouse. As an experienced operator, HANDLEMAN will dress and comport himself unobtrusively so as not to attract undue attention. The apartment building will, if possible, have multiple unmanned entrances. HANDLEMAN will arrive first, check for any anomalies and, if everything looks okay, will leave a safety signal of some sort right outside the door of the apartment. Again, since it is not a face-to-face public contact, the situation is somewhat reversed in that it will be the agent, not the clandestine operator, who will initiate the contact, and it will be the clandestine operator who will display the safety signal. HOPEWARS/1, who will have left his own home on a satisfactory pretext that satisfies his wife, will then arrive, knock, be admitted by HANDLEMAN, and they will hold a meeting. If interrupted, or if they have to explain what they are doing there, they will say that they are waiting for the woman whose apartment it is. They don't even have to give her name because such women often use assumed names with clients.

The cover story is somewhat weak, to be sure. It might work with local people and even with law enforcement, but is less likely to work with the professional counterintelligence opposition which is unlikely to be fooled when coming upon a military officer meeting with a foreigner in such a situation. However, while weak as a cover, it still does provide a fig-leaf of sorts, and both must stick to that cover if only for legal reasons.

Although it is true that such a cover story might not hold up with the professional opposition, especially in an authoritarian country, it is important to understand that the main goal of cover, concealment, and compartmentation is to preclude the participants, and their mutual contact from ever coming to the attention of the opposition. The local professional counterintelligence service controls the environment with lots of authority. Once they start to scrutinize these activities, it usually means that the operation is dead even if they don't get "the goods" on you. Many an amateur will say, oh, if caught we can always say such and such. But once you're caught, the operation is over, even if your cover explanation does hold up legally.

But now that HANDLEMAN and HOPEWARS/1 have established a regular meeting scenario, HANDLEMAN will gradually start inculcating the rest of the paraphernalia necessary for a productive and secure clandestine relationship between a sponsoring clandestine organization and a secret agent. They will establish alternate meeting arrangements in case a regular meeting is interrupted or aborted; they will settle on means of triggering non-scheduled meetings in urgent situations, and agree on re-contact procedures in case a clandestine operator unknown to HOPEWARS/1 has to re-establish contact with him.

Eventually, HANDLEMAN will train HOPEWARS/1 in non-personal methods of communication which would obviate the need for HANDLEMAN to meet his agent face-to-face in his own country. But before HOPEWARS/1 can be left to report information on his own, the next order of business is to teach him the art of reporting on political, economic, and military matters of interest to the sponsoring clandestine organization and to its customers.

CHAPTER VI

Information Reporting

HOPEWARS/1 is now back in Degenera, his home country. Clandestine operator HANDLEMAN and his clandestine organization are delighted that HOPEWARS/1 has been assigned to a staff position on the Joint High General Staff of Degenera's military establishment. The sponsoring clandestine organization has long wanted a reliable secret-agent penetration of Degenera's military, and it now wants to exploit HOPEWARS/1's access to non-public Degeneran military information.

But there is much to be done to make HOPEWARS/1 a truly good secret reporting agent. He is now going to have to do more than merely supply personality information on his non-Degeneran colleagues and contacts, or provide his clandestine operator with rumors or circumstantial material as he did back in Probahlia where he was a third-country diplomatic attache dealing with the Probahlian military. Now he is being tasked to provide substantive factual information about Degenera itself, of which he has direct personal knowledge through his work.

He has shown a willingness to do so, but his understanding of information reporting needs improvement.

A Not-Uncommon Conversation with an Inexperienced Agent

To better understand some of the principles of information reporting, let us consider the following conversation at a clandestine meeting on October 19 between clandestine operator HANDLEMAN and his secret agent HOPEWARS/1, who is still somewhat inexperienced as a reporter.

HOPEWARS/1:	I have some information for you. You can be sure that the Republic of Guardia intends to invade Probahlia very shortly, probably within a week.
HANDLEMAN:	How do you know this?
HOPEWARS/1:	Because Colonel Ambro Gasfullia of the Degeneran Army said so in a staff meeting.
HANDLEMAN:	How do you know?
HOPEWARS/1:	I was at the meeting as the official note-taker.
HANDLEMAN:	Do you remember when the meeting took place?
HOPEWARS/1:	It was at the Monday morning staff meeting, yesterday October 18.
HANDLEMAN:	Did Colonel Gasfullia say how he knew that such an invasion will be taking place?

HOPEWARS/1: He said that the week before, he and his wife had been on vacation at a Guardia resort hotel in the river-town of Salatio. He said that every morning after breakfast he took a stroll along the Sewage River, which is the border between Probahlia and Guardia, and one morning he saw about twenty-five segments of military pontoon bridges stacked on the river bank and they had not been there the day before.

HANDLEMAN: Why does that mean that Guardia is about to invade Probahlia?

HOPEWARS/1: Due to humidity and possible rusting, these bridge segments would never be left out in that tropical climate unless they were intended for immediate use.

HANDLEMAN: Did the Colonel actually say that he himself believed that an invasion is imminent?

HOPEWARS/1: No, but it's obvious that's what he meant. What other reason would the Guardians have for stacking these bridges in readiness?

HANDLEMAN: Did the Colonel say that he saw other similar bridge segments stacked elsewhere along the river?

HOPEWARS/1: He didn't say.

HANDLEMAN: Were there any Guardian military personnel around?

HOPEWARS/1: The Colonel didn't say.

HANDLEMAN: Why would Guardia want to invade Probahlia?

HOPEWARS/1:   There is a dispute between Guardia and Probahlia over the Eastern Swamp territory which both countries claim. In fact, several months ago I told our mutual friend SHARPERSON in Probahlia that Probahlia decided not to participate with Degenera in joint military exercises so as not to antagonize Guardia which might see the exercises as a direct threat to itself due to the Eastern Swamp dispute.

HANDLEMAN: Well, I thank you, my friend. This is very useful. Please keep an eye out for additional information on this topic.

HOPEWARS/1:   I will. Meanwhile, tell your people that Guardia is about to invade Probahlia.

Many would conclude that the foregoing information from HOPEWARS/1 constitutes "intelligence" that Guardia is about to invade Probahlia. Actually, it is nothing of the sort. To be sure, it is information that might <u>suggest</u> a coming invasion, but it has to be analyzed in conjunction with other information before it becomes "intelligence" indicating that an invasion might actually take place.

In order to understand the foregoing better, it is necessary to consider just what, specifically, HOPEWARS/1 is reporting from his own direct knowledge. The only real fact that he knows is that an officer of the Degeneran Ministry of Defense told him and his colleagues that he noted the presence of military pontoon bridges stacked outdoors in Guardia along the river frontier with Probahlia and that the officer believes that it is indicative of a coming invasion. That is ALL that HOPEWARS/1 himself knows, and when you get right down to it, it is ALL that he is reporting. Everything else is inference. It is incumbent on HANDLEMAN when reporting his meeting with HOPEWARS/1 that he make sure that the facts that HOPEWARS/1 reported are clearly separated from any opinions, inferences, and analysis.

Before anyone concludes that an invasion will actually take place, the customers (i.e. the policy makers and analysts) will consider other information as well, such as the state of readiness and the capabilities of the Guardian armed forces, past attitudes of Guardian leaders in similar circumstances, Guardian diplomatic initiatives with Probahlia and with other countries, information from other sources on communication between Probahlian and Guardian diplomats, and information from state-run media in all three countries, as well as diplomatic discussions between HANDLEMAN's own country and Degenera, Guardia, and Probahlia. The conclusion then might well be that an invasion is highly unlikely and that the presence of the pontoon bridges on the riverbank has no serious significance.

With the foregoing in mind, we now come to the all-important difference between "information" and "intelligence," a difference which ALL clandestine operators MUST understand if they want to be true professionals.

Information versus Intelligence

Separating information from intelligence is a classical skill of spycraft. Even customers and sponsors of espionage (such as George Washington) have traditionally used the words "intelligence" and "information" interchangeably, but there has always been a difference, which today's professionals often delineate by the different words. Simply put, "intelligence" contains "information" after the information has been studied in conjunction with other information, and has been collated, synthesized and analyzed to arrive at conclusions.

The foregoing point is of such importance to the professional mentality of a clandestine operator that I will emphasize it by citing another example from my earlier book, *My CIA:Memories of a Secret Career*. It hypothesizes a similar case that suggests impending hostilities between the fictitious countries of Aggressia and Defendia:

Let us say there is a report that in <u>February</u> a memorandum was circulating in the Ministry of Defense of the Republic of Aggressia that earlier, in <u>January</u>, Aggressia's president, Mango Finosit, had stated at a cabinet meeting that he wanted his army to prepare for an invasion next <u>May</u> of the neighboring Kingdom of Defendia. Many will conclude that the foregoing report constitutes "intelligence" that Aggressia intends to invade Defendia in May.

We need to analyze the information in conjunction with other information. For example, what do we know about President Finosit's policies and attitudes regarding Defendia? Can we acquire information perhaps from other sources that will help us understand whether Aggressia's leadership truly believes that such an invasion would succeed? Is such an invasion feasible? Do we have information about any Aggressian government efforts behind the scenes to seek support from friendly governments? Might the president's orders to prepare an invasion merely be a military exercise, or a test of preparedness, or only a bluff? What, precisely, does the information report really convey?

In the foregoing example, one cannot emphasize too strongly that the *only* thing the information actually conveys is that, in February, a memorandum was circulating saying that in January the president of Aggressia had ordered preparations for an invasion to take place in May. It is important to understand that the date of the foregoing information is <u>February</u>, which is when the memorandum was circulating, for that is the <u>only thing</u> that the agent who reported it to us knows directly.

Therefore, the date of the foregoing information is not January, when the president allegedly made his statement, for the source has no direct knowledge of that fact. And the date of information is certainly not May, which is when the alleged invasion is supposed to take place. Future events haven't happened yet, so they do not constitute facts. Information can <u>never</u> have a future date.

All this might strike the reader as an exposition on the obvious, but it is not obvious to many people. Governments, corporations, and individuals frequently make dumb decisions by relying on snippets of information without analyzing them with respect to other information or to the bigger picture. Thus they fail to grasp the intelligence regarding a situation and are unable to judge the probability of a future event.

People can always dredge up some bit of information that "proves" that (for example) Roosevelt knew that the attack on Pearl Harbor was about to take place. Or that the State Department knew that Fidel Castro was a communist but was initially friendly toward him anyway. Or that George W. Bush knew that 9/11 was going to take place, but let it happen nevertheless. Or that he knew that there were no weapons of mass destruction in Iraq, but wanted an excuse for war.

Anyone with any experience in the intelligence profession knows that in any situation there is some information that, taken by itself, suggests one or another possibility. Anyone - an unscrupulous journalist, a self-serving legislator, or a politically motivated government bureaucrat - can selectively pull out those bits of unanalyzed information and present it as "intelligence" in support of whatever perception he or she favors."

Analysis of information from public sources and also secret sources might indicate that it is unlikely that Aggressia is about to attack Defendia, and indicate instead that the Aggressian government intends to make public its preparation for an invasion as a saber-rattling gesture, and that, in reality, Aggressia has a shortage of fuel that actually precludes an invasion of Defendia at that time. Thus, the resulting intelligence indicates that information alleging Aggressia's preparation for an invasion is merely a public gesture and not a real invasion plan. Such ***intelligence*** is often quite different from what the individual piece of ***information*** might have suggested.

The original information report might also generate new questions and new requests for yet more information. Such new questions and requests are known as "information requirements" (often misleadingly called "intelligence requirements"). The sponsoring clandestine organization will try to satisfy the new requirements in its future reporting. This brings us to a related concept known as the Intelligence Cycle.

The Intelligence Cycle

The foregoing underscores a sequential process that goes like this: 1) The clandestine organization's customer poses certain questions known as "requirements;" 2) the sponsoring organization then collects secret information (and non-clandestine government organizations will collect non-secret information) to help respond to the customer's request; 3) intelligence analysts then collate the information; 4) synthesize it; and 5) analyze it, thereby producing an intelligence report. They then 6) disseminate the report to the customer which then 7) provides feedback; and 8) formulates new requirements.

The sequence of events thus described is known as the ***intelligence cycle*** and it behooves every clandestine operator to understand it well. I repeat that it begins with the needs of the customer (usually a government) in the form of "intelligence requirements." Those requirements lead to the collection of information that might help answer the customer's questions. The information must be organized, brought together, and analyzed into what is called "intelligence," which is a careful factual conclusion in response to the customer's questions. The intelligence then often generates new questions "or requirements" from the customer. And so, the cycle renews itself. (See Figure 9.)

Again, we see that information and intelligence are not the same thing. "Information" comes in bits and pieces from various sources of widely differing access and reliability, some of it overt and some of it acquired covertly. It is often contradictory and misleading. It can come from overt sources like newspapers, or radio and TV broadcasts, or it can come from conversations between officials of two countries, or else from clandestine sources like electronic intercepts, or secret agents. All such information must be collated, synthesized, and analyzed in order to produce what we call "intelligence," which is really a conclusion made from many inputs of information.

PRODUCTION OF INTELLIGENCE

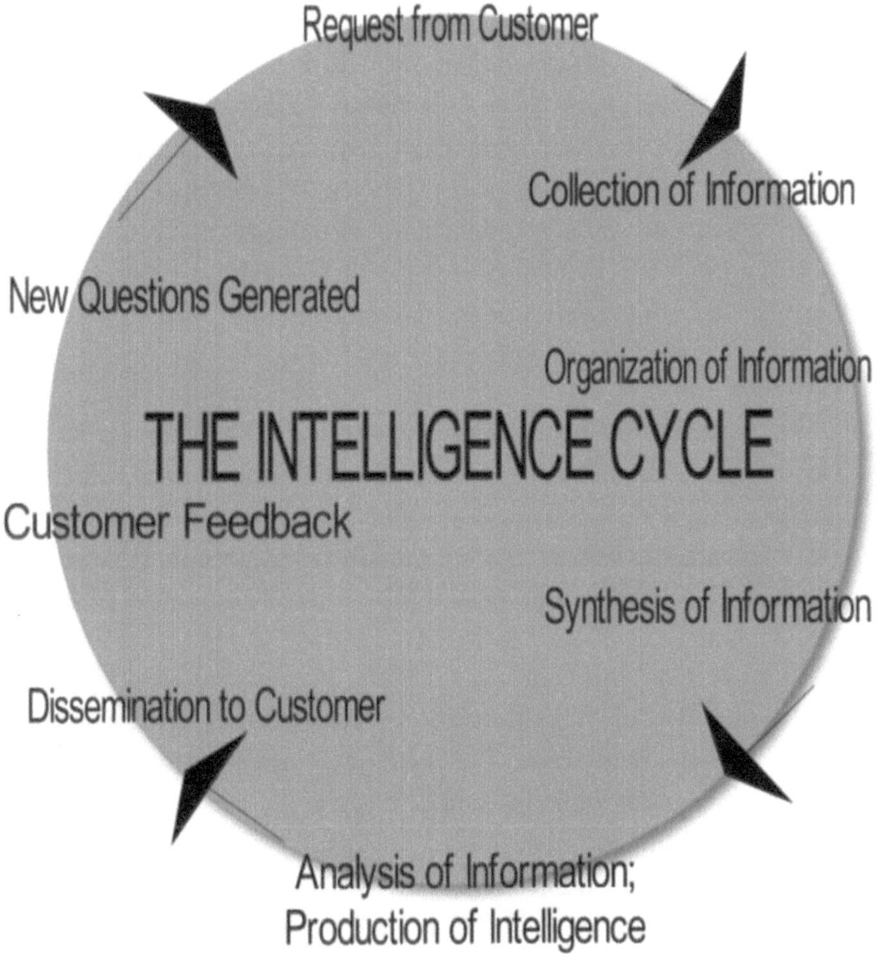

Figure 9

An important aspect of the intelligence cycle is that any participant may enter it at any point. Not only may the customer initiate requirements, but a clandestine operator might learn of new information that is not necessarily in response to a specific customer-requirement but which the operator judges might be of significance. Such information would enter the cycle, be organized and synthesized with other information, and disseminated to the customer, who may or may not generate new requirements about it. Ditto, an analyst might produce an analysis outlining the consequences of new public or semi-public information, and place it into the cycle as a new report, which might generate new requirements for clandestine collection.

One can now see that the reporting of information gleaned from espionage requires a strictly rigorous "left brained" approach, or as others might put it, the application of one's neo-cortex rather than the reptilian and glandular portion of one's mind. This should also be true of good journalists and law enforcement personnel. As Sergeant Friday used to say on television, "Just the facts ma'am."

Therefore, a clandestine organization, in collecting information, must eschew all classical logical errors such as mixing fact with inference, circular reasoning, causal oversimplifications, unwarranted analogies, false dichotomies, unjustified extrapolations, and so forth. These and other pitfalls might earn someone an ignoble living through bad journalism or unscrupulous politics, but have no place in the espionage business. There is no room for mushy thinking when reporting information that one acquires clandestinely.

Despite the foregoing, and despite the care that a clandestine organization might take to separate fact from inference, there will always be (alas) some people who will read the information from HOPEWARS/1 as "intelligence" that Guardia is about to invade Probahlia, or that Aggressia is about to attack Defendia. And, when the invasion or attack fails to take place, they will call it "bad intelligence" or an "intelligence failure," even if the informational content is actually true.

Or else they will cherry-pick factual information that tends to support their pre-conceptions, and will ignore the rest that militate against their pre-conceptions. Such misinterpretation on the part of the customers of a clandestine organization is the frequent bane of those who earn their living by acquiring factual information clandestinely.

It should be clear from HANDLEMAN's conversation with HOPEWARS/1, which generated the first example cited above, that HANDLEMAN has to engage in detailed questioning to extract information from HOPEWARS/1 in a coherent factual form that might be of use to intelligence analysts in formulating an intelligence finding. HOPEWARS/1 is clearly not quite ready for impersonal communication through written messages, and will not be ready until he absorbs the basic principles of information reporting.

In addition, before the clandestine organization allows HOPEWARS/1 to gather information and to report it without supervision, the agent's clandestine operator must not only ensure his intellectual training as a factual reporter, but must also vet the agent thoroughly as trustworthy and reliable. The vetting requires minute attention to the counterintelligence aspects of his relationship with the sponsoring clandestine organization. For this reason, a full understanding of counterintelligence is also an essential tool for the clandestine operator.

CHAPTER VII

Counterintelligence And Agent Handling

By ***counterintelligence*** I mean the <u>defensive</u> efforts of a clandestine or security organization to counter and detect foreign clandestine activity, and thereby protect itself and its customers.

By ***counterespionage*** I mean the <u>offensive</u> efforts of a clandestine or security organization to spy specifically against a hostile intelligence or security organizations. Its purpose is to learn the opposing organization's techniques and operations, and thereby further protect itself.

Obviously, counterespionage is part of an overall counterintelligence effort, so there is a tendency to employ the word "counterintelligence" even when we are referring specifically to counterespionage. Even professionals often use the terms interchangeably. However, to better understand this chapter, the reader will do well to grasp the difference.

Any operation that specifically targets a clandestine operation, rather than merely tries to detect it and defend against it, is a counterespionage operation. Counterespionage operations carried out by a clandestine or security organization against inimical organizations are much like information-collection operations against other targets on behalf of its customers. The main difference is that when a clandestine organization engages in counterespionage to collect information about another clandestine organization, <u>it is its own customer</u> since the information is primarily a benefit to itself.

Internal and External Services

Most nations have two separate clandestine capabilities. These are embodied in an "internal service" and an "external service." The internal service is generally responsible for protecting a nation against foreign clandestine operations and, as such, is a counterintelligence service. It usually works within its own country. The external service is the clandestine organization responsible for carrying out espionage and other clandestine activities abroad against foreign targets.

Classic examples are the FBI (an internal service) which operates in America, and the CIA's Clandestine Service (an external service) which operates abroad. Other examples are the historic MI-5 and MI-6 organizations in Britain. In the Soviet Union during the Cold War there were distinct departments in each of the two main Soviet services (the KGB and GRU) which carried out separate internal and external functions.

But the foregoing can be very misleading. It should not imply that an external service, operating clandestinely abroad against foreign targets, carries out <u>solely</u> defensive counterintelligence precautions with regard to its clandestine operations. In actuality it may also carry out counterespionage activities against intelligence services operating against it abroad. The reason is not only to further protect its own clandestine operations, but also because such counterespionage abroad would be beyond the scope of its country's internal service back home.

It might seem sufficient for a clandestine organization operating abroad to guard against a counterintelligence threat by simply applying cover, concealment and compartmentation to the degree necessary to thwart the local professional counterintelligence opposition. But such a passive, defensive posture would be considerably enhanced by an offensive, aggressive counterespionage activity to target the local counterintelligence opposition. Indeed, the latter counterintelligence opposition might itself carry out counterespionage activity against your clandestine organization, and can often be extremely clever in gaining control of your clandestine operations and using them against your clandestine organization.

A classic counterespionage ploy against a clandestine organization is known as the ***dangle***.

Dangles

At the very outset, whenever a clandestine operator seeks a new secret agent abroad, he has to be careful that the professional opposition (i.e. the local counterintelligence service), or some other hostile organization, isn't engaging in counterespionage and dangling someone under its control as bait in the hope that you will recruit him. If that happens, you can end up recruiting a person as a secret agent whom the other side is really controlling, and through whom the other side can learn a great deal about your own organization.

If that were to happen, the other side would learn a great deal about the doctrines, personnel, methods, techniques, and capabilities of your own clandestine organization. Another reason might be to feed you false and misleading information. Yet another reason might be to tie up your local manpower and cause your own clandestine organization to waste its resources.

Even if a clandestine operator is very cautious and manifests a good counterintelligence attitude, the need for utter objectivity requires a well-managed clandestine organization to maintain an excellent counterintelligence component to scrutinize all operations, particularly new recruitments, for signs of counterespionage efforts by the other side, and thereby minimize the possibility that a hostile foreign hand might be behind them. In order to ensure such objectivity, the counterintelligence component should be somewhat removed from those who are actually carrying out operations.

It is a truism that clandestine operators who acquire and handle secret agents tend to attach the most positive interpretations to the behavior of their agents, while counterintelligence personnel tend to interpret everything in the most negative way. This leads to a certain tension between the clandestine operators and counterintelligence personnel within their own organization. It is a tension that on balance is healthful.

For example, in the case of SHARPERSON's recruitment of HOPEWARS/1, one would naturally expect SHARPERSON and his immediate superiors to wax enthusiastic regarding the development of a secret relationship with a well-placed asset such as HOPEWARS/1. But the counterintelligence people in SHARPERSON's clandestine organization would have some suspicions and misgivings. They might wonder whether the evolution of HOPEWARS/1, first as SHARPERSON's personal friend and sometime casual provider of information regarding a third country, then to that of a systematic and paid provider of such information, and finally to a treasonable provider of information on his own country, might have happened too quickly and too neatly.

Indeed, when HOPEWARS/1 shifted from his role as an agent who was spying against a third country to an agent spying against his own country, the shift moved faster than one would expect, and would certainly raise some red flags among those supervising SHARPERSON. They might debate whether HOPEWARS/1 was, from the very beginning, working for an opposition service against SHARPERSON's clandestine organization, and was therefore "dangled" as bait. These misgivings might eventually be resolved by a detailed and cold-blooded assessment of how SHARPERSON and HOPEWARS/1 originally met, and an analysis of the real value of HOPEWARS/1's information as passed to SHARPERSON. SHARPERSON's organization would want to be reasonably comfortable about HOPEWARS/1 before exposing a new clandestine operator to him (in this case HANDLEMAN) when HOPEWARS/1 returns to his home country Degenera.

Walk-Ins

Perhaps the most obvious possibility of a dangle is what is called a ***walk-in***, which is anyone who, without any personal development by a clandestine operator, approaches a clandestine organization and offers his services. It can be someone who walks into a foreign embassy, or into a foreign business office, or who in any way offers himself to one's own country and organization.

Needless to say, walk-ins are always suspect even if their potential is great. Sometimes they are indeed under the control of the professional opposition. The reasons for sending a walk-in can vary. Sometimes an opposition service wants to learn your service's protocol for handling such situations, or wants to flush out the identities of the clandestine operators inside a cover organization, be it an embassy or a corporation, since it is likely that a clandestine operator will be the one who will be assigned to deal with the walk-in.

One motive might be to run a **screen operation** designed to sap the time and resources of a clandestine organization by waving operational possibilities in front of its personnel; possibilities that require much attention such as bomb threats or misleading information as to military action against the clandestine organization's customer country or its allies.

Sometimes they hope that the receiving organization will be fooled, and that the walk-in can then feed it false information over a protracted period. But the latter is not as frequent a motive for sending a walk-in against you, because the professional opposition well knows that you are also professional, and that your service will examine the walk-in closely and that you are not likely to be fooled in the long run.

Altogether too often, there is actually nobody controlling a walk-in except himself. This is particularly true at official government installations, such as foreign embassies, when someone who considers himself clever "walks in" on his own initiative with a proposal with which he thinks he can milk money from the foreign government. Such ploys usually don't work. Such walk-ins are rarely smart enough or knowledgeable enough to pull it off, nor are clandestine organizations so inept as to fall for such ploys.

Compromise and Counter-Recruitment

Probably the most devastating counterintelligence threat is when a good agent goes sour. This can occur for a number of reasons.

Sometimes an agent who has been recruited solely on the basis of his venality decides to supplement his income by offering himself to another service as well. It would not necessarily be his own country's service, which would likely take a jaundiced view of his treason. It might be a third-country service that is eager to learn about your organization or else has an interest in deceiving you for a number of different reasons. Or else, your agent has been discovered, and his country's service decides to run him back against you, either to deceive you with false information or to learn more about your methods, about your personnel, and about your service's infrastructure such as safehouses, technical capabilities, and other aspects.

Sometimes the doubling-back operation is inspired by the agent's resentment or desire for revenge. That is why in the recruitment process it is very unwise to use coercive pressure based on a potential agent's vulnerabilities, and instead use positive inducements aimed at the target's susceptibilities. Reluctant agents who are coerced are bad agents.

Assessing and Justifying a Secret Agent

The simplest and best way to assess the legitimacy of a secret agent is by constant evaluation of the information he gives you. This is particularly true with regard to information that a walk-in offers to prove his legitimacy and his good faith as a source. Such initial information is sometimes called **bona fides**.

In the case of a walk-in, detailed questioning by an experienced operator, combined with research in the files on the topics contained in the information he offers, can often reveal whether a walk-in is truthful as to who he is and as to the access and capabilities that he claims to have. In the case of a recruited secret agent, the development and recruitment process must have included background investigation and detailed assessment that would have already yielded a picture of who he is, his potential usefulness, his motivation, his susceptibilities and his vulnerabilities.

A detailed analysis and assessment of such an agent's information can eventually reveal whether he is really producing the sort of information that the other side wishes to keep secret, or whether it is merely "throw-away" material designed to deceive the recipient. But in a carefully-managed double-agent operation, it is not always certain.

In my book *My CIA: Memories of a Secret Career*, I recounted a case that spanned several countries. A hostile service had ostensibly recruited a foreigner whose job brought him to a number of official American installations abroad in a number of countries. He came to us, told us of his recruitment, and offered his services to us instead. We ran him as a counterespionage **double agent,** which means he was working ostensibly as an agent for the other side, but had really become an agent for us against them. We met with him regularly in various places as he traveled around the world. Through him, we thought we were learning a great deal about the espionage methodology of the other side. Also, through him, we fed the other side bogus information about the installations he visited.

We also learned the identities of numerous hostile clandestine operators who handled the agent in the various countries he visited, and who worked undercover in their country's embassies. Those identities constituted a particularly important trove of valuable information because it told us which officers in hostile installations were engaged in clandestine activities, and on whom we should focus in the future when they appeared and reappeared in various places abroad. It was considered a successful and useful double-agent operation.

Then word came down from the head of our service that the operation should be allowed to peter out. In a meeting in his office, he announced that after a thorough counterintelligence analysis it had emerged that every hostile clandestine operator identified through the operation had been on a list of that service's espionage trainees that one of our agent penetrations of that service had passed to us many years earlier. Years before, the hostile clandestine service had eventually detected and arrested our penetration, so his contribution to us was obviously known to the other side. The operation, which was taking up a lot of our time and resources, was clearly yielding a lot of information already in our files. We had been victims of a screen operation designed to tie up our resources, and which revealed to the other side more than it revealed to us.

We have noted earlier that not only might a clandestine operator be the target of a hostile dangle or a bogus walk-in; it is also possible for good and productive agents to turn sour later for a number of reasons, and then betray a clandestine operator or his organization to an opposing service. There are therefore certain counterintelligence practices to be followed to minimize the foregoing possibility.

Counterintelligence in Agent Handling

Of course, every clandestine operator should be sensitive to the possibility that one or more of his agents may be doubled against him at the outset. That is why in our original spotting and assessment reports there must be an evaluation of his susceptibilities and vulnerabilities, not solely to help us decide the best approach, but to glean an idea of the person's potential attractiveness to other services. And, since an agent might later go sour, a clandestine operator must constantly test his agents, assess their demeanor and attitudes, and never fail to exercise discipline and control. Here are some of the basic counterespionage elements on which a clandestine operator must focus when handling agents:

<u>SUSCEPTIBILITIES:</u> We have discussed susceptibilities in great detail earlier in this book, and indeed they serve as a basis for recruiting a secret agent. Suffice it to remind the reader that if an agent is susceptible to recruitment by you, he could also be susceptible to recruitment by others. This might be less so if his motivation is ideological, but more so if his motivation is venal or ego gratification.

<u>VULNERABILITIES:</u> As mentioned, this is information that protects the clandestine operator by rendering it less

likely that a recruit would report a recruitment attempt to his superiors lest the "dirt" on him emerge when doing so. But, vulnerability information regarding other matters not related to an agent's relationship with the clandestine operator is also a counterintelligence factor, since it might attract the scrutiny of the agent by other intelligence or police services.

As we said, although a number of intelligence services might use vulnerabilities to coerce an agent, good operational practices dictate against it. As a tool to generate cooperation, it creates problems. Simply put, a reluctant, resentful, coerced agent is all too often a bad agent - an agent that might be constantly seeking a way to turn against you.

The foregoing is not necessarily true when an internal counterintelligence service, or a police service, is seeking sources and is operating within its own country. After all, a police or internal service controls the operating environment. Its personnel and their sources do not have to worry about their own arrest or expulsion if they are compromised, and these services are in a position to squeeze their sources with less subtlety for more and better information, and to demand more meticulous discipline and greater effort.

But long experience indicates that an external service operating in a foreign country simply cannot afford to run a resentful or disaffected agent. Instead, a good clandestine operator should make every effort to bind his agent closer to him with mutual respect, with reward more than chastisement, and will try to make the agent feel like a member of a team that is solicitous of his welfare. That is why, for counterintelligence reasons, the clandestine operator must devote time for rapport in his meetings with his agents, in accordance with the doctrine mentioned earlier on the structure of agent meetings.

AGENT TESTING: Regardless of how much a clandestine operator trusts his agents, he must test them as much as possible and as often as possible. Every meeting should contain collection or action requirements, even if such requirements are not important to you, and even if you already have such information from other sources. In fact, it is particularly useful to glean information from your agent even if you have the information from another source, as this creates a basis for evaluating the usefulness and honesty of both sources. An agent should never lie fallow. He should always be kept busy, accustomed to doing your bidding, and accustomed to reaping the rewards for doing so. Also, if he is ever compromised and forced to reveal the "requirements" levied on him, those "requirements" which in actuality had already been serviced by your other sources might deceive his interrogators as to how much you really know already.

ASSESSMENT OF DEMEANOR AND ATTITUDE: A clandestine operator MUST constantly have his counterintelligence "antennae" tuned, and must always carefully observe and assess the comportment of his agents. Again, that is why the rapport part of an agent-meeting is so important.

The clandestine operator should make it evident to his agents that the foundation of their relationship with his clandestine sponsoring organization is the organization's sincere concern for them and their welfare, and that it is also the sincere concern of the clandestine operator who manages them. The concern should focus on the agent's security, his satisfaction, and his welfare. Such concern must not come across as contrived. If it does come across as insincere, the clandestine operator should not be surprised later to discern a certain lack of responsiveness on the part of the agent and, worse, a possible diminishment in the quality, quantity, or reliability of his reporting or his activities.

AGENT DISCIPLINE AND CONTROL: The foregoing does not mean that the clandestine operator should diminish strict control over his agent. He must inculcate adherence to security procedures and protocols, as well as timeliness and reliability of information reported. And he must discourage security weaknesses such as attention-getting behavior in his agent's social life such as ostentatious spending. But, as mentioned, the operator must do this always in the context of the agent's welfare, security, and prosperity. The clandestine operator can push for better production, more objective reporting, and demand greater pains in accuracy and thoroughness, but should do so in the context of justifying greater rewards and remuneration for the agent.

When it comes to control and discipline, one must discourage the tendency that one sometimes sees in clandestine operators who are former law enforcement officials or military personnel to indulge in the habits of their previous authoritarian careers when trying to control or impose discipline on their agents. When operating in a country not one's own, the clandestine operator is in no position to castigate, mortify, bully, or restrain his agent. He cannot put his agent in jail, or in the stockade, or in the brig, nor can he make his life miserable by legal harassment, nor can he demand some sort of adherence on the basis of the clandestine operator's rank or position. Both of you are doing illegal things in the operating environment, and your agent can seriously damage you if he decides to do it. So, a clandestine operator must exercise discipline and control primarily through positive reinforcement rather than by negative stimulus. I repeat: a disaffected or reluctant or resentful agent is a bad and dangerous agent.

In Sum

We have seen that after HOPEWARS/1's recruitment, the clandestine operator SHARPERSON and his successor HANDLEMAN had to train HOPEWARS/1 in the practice of operational security and in the principles of information reporting. Such training, as we have noted, is in bits and pieces rather than all at once so as not to overload the agent or induce in him any second thoughts as to what he has gotten himself into. HOPEWARS/1's clandestine operator will continue to train him whenever new procedures are necessary to service collection requirements, or if there are changes in security or communication requirements.

I reiterate that it is necessary to keep an agent busy by continuously tasking him, even with respect to information or activity that is of little interest to you. We do this not only so he will stay responsive to his clandestine operator and to the clandestine organization, but also to bury the clandestine organization's real interests among less important tasks in order to confuse the opposition in the event of the agent's compromise, and mislead the opposition as to what the clandestine organization already knows or doesn't know

Furthermore, tasking an agent for information that the clandestine organization already knows serves as a counterintelligence check of his veracity and reliability. In the area of counterintelligence, it is imperative that an agent's clandestine operators constantly assess an agent's motivation, loyalty, changes in demeanor, and possible disaffection. It is very important that although one has developed a relationship with an agent all the way to recruitment, his clandestine operators must continue developing him throughout the life of the operation in order to strengthen his ties to the organization as much as possible.

We can then summarize in a nutshell the agent handling practices elucidated so far: Training, Tasking, Testing, Assessing, and Continued Development; the last three being particularly relevant to counterintelligence. (Figure 10.)

Agent Termination

There are times when an agent is no longer cost-effective in terms of money spent on him, or time dedicated to managing him. Or else the clandestine organization has a diminished interest in his particular access to information or other capabilities. Or simply that the agent is unmanageable in terms of security and is no longer worth the risk of running him. In such a case, it becomes necessary to terminate him.

The obvious problem inherent in letting any agent go is akin to the problem inherent in a dangle. A terminated agent who is no longer bound to your organization and over whom you no longer have any control could, as in the case of a dangle, compromise a great deal about the doctrines, personnel, methods, techniques, and capabilities of your own clandestine organization. The only difference is that a dangle does not initially have information on such matters pertaining to your organization, but the former agent does have such knowledge through his long association with you!!

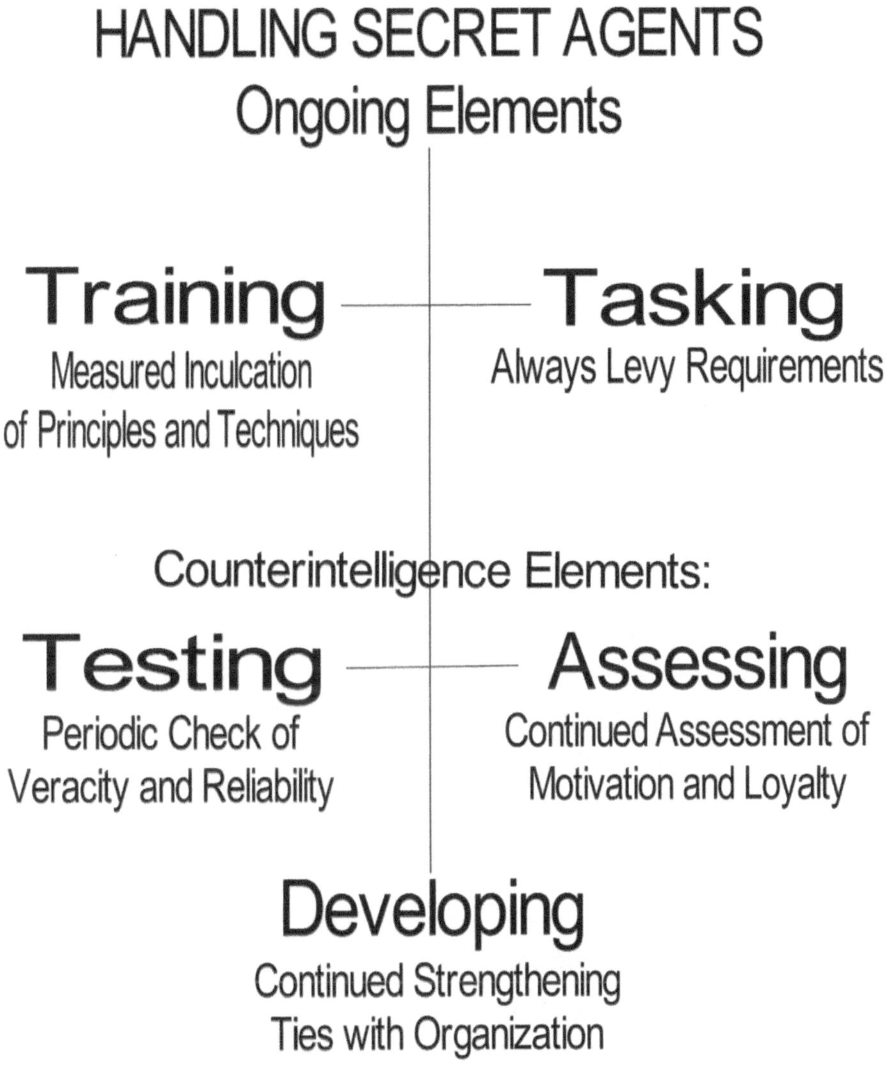
HANDLING SECRET AGENTS
Ongoing Elements
Training
Measured Inculcation of Principles and Techniques
Tasking
Always Levy Requirements
Counterintelligence Elements:
Testing
Periodic Check of Veracity and Reliability
Assessing
Continued Assessment of Motivation and Loyalty
Developing
Continued Strengthening Ties with Organization

Figure 10

Another potential compromise that many people fail to consider involves our opposition's potential knowledge of our information-collection requirements, which a former agent might know in detail. If our enemies know we are asking for details about (as a fictitious example that I gave in my book, ***My CIA: Memories of a Secret Career***) their new special training activity on Al-Barren Mountain, someone high up on the other side might ask, "How could the Americans know anything about that? The only ones besides me who know about it are Ali Mustafa, Mohamed Herzi, and Ahmed Suleiman. Hmmm…I wonder. . .". And shortly afterward our source will be toast. Clearly, knowledge as to what a clandestine organization does not know is often dangerously entwined with information as to what it does know.

Termination of an agent does not in real life have the sinister implication that it has in spy movies. It is merely the termination of employment, albeit with some unique counterintelligence risks illustrated above. Obviously, no clandestine organization relishes having a former agent, over whom it no longer has any contact or control, wandering around bitter and angry while possessing a trove of knowledge about the service, its personnel, its procedures and its intelligence needs. That is why a clandestine organization, after making a detailed counterintelligence analysis of a given situation, may elect to continue running such an agent even if he is no longer useful or effective.

That's why, if the organization decides that termination is in order, the clandestine operator clearly ought to do everything possible for the foregoing reasons to make sure that the agent does not feel criticized, disciplined, disrespected, or rejected. Instead, the termination should proceed in a manner that leaves the agent as satisfied and as happy as possible, with expressions of gratitude, and with gifts and emoluments which, one would hope, would generate some sort of residual loyalty to his former employer.

Singleton Agents versus Networks

In general, when a clandestine operator handles a number of different agents who are unknown to each other, they are called singletons. When they are known to each other and interact with each other, they are a network. Throughout history, clandestine operators have debated the pros and cons of running single agents versus networks of agents who are in contact with one another.

Singleton operations are better protected because the agents are run individually and are compartmented from each other. If one agent is compromised, it would not lead to the compromise of the others. One could argue, however, that even if a clandestine operator runs a series of compartmented singleton agents and he himself is compromised, he might be forced to identify his other agents. But the foregoing danger can be mitigated somewhat if the agent does not know the identity of the clandestine operator who handles him. Such anonymity would be a worthy goal after the original recruiter, whom the agent of course knows, eventually turns him over to someone else for handling, who might operate in alias or disguise. Furthermore, the clandestine organization should enhance the operational security of a clandestine operator who is handling a number of singleton agents by ensuring that the status cover of such a clandestine operator in the country be low profile, that he handle only tried and trusted agents, and that he not engage in risky activities such as agent recruitment.

But if the agents are known to each other, and if they form what is often called an "espionage ring," the danger to all of them from the compromise of just one of them is obvious, whether the clandestine operator himself is compromised or not, since the clandestine organization would be unable to prevent one of the compromised agents from revealing other elements of the whole network. In general, well-managed clandestine organizations are leery of networks except in such unavoidable situations as surveillance teams whose members must work together.

In my particular operational philosophy, a clandestine operator should handle all his agents as singletons, even if the risk of scrutiny might be minimal when all are buried deeply in local society. But it might tempt the operator, in order to make their activities less cumbersome and time consuming, to allow his agents to become aware of each other, and to communicate with each other and with him through different channels. This is especially true if the agents knew each other personally before they became agents. But such a lack of compartmentation would add considerable risk to the whole group in the event of the compromise of any one element.

Classic Cases: The Rosenberg and Sorge Networks

Examples of buried, deep-cover networks are the famous Rosenberg network in the US, and the Sorge network in Japan, both during the 1940s. Both networks were for a time spectacularly successful. The Rosenberg ring in the U.S. provided the Soviets with critical information regarding radar, sonar, jet propulsion and nuclear technology at a time when the US was the only country in the world that possessed it. The Sorge ring in Japan was able to collect information indicating almost with certainty that the Japanese would not attack the Soviet Union in the east, thereby allowing Stalin to concentrate more forces in the west against Germany. But both espionage rings would have lasted longer if not for fundamental flaws in compartmentation which allowed the counterintelligence opposition to dismantle their activities.

Regarding the Rosenberg ring, Julius and Ethel Rosenberg recruited members of their family and circle of friends to act as information-collecting agents. Julius reported to a Soviet clandestine operator who was under official cover and whom he, of course, met secretly. At the same time, another Rosenberg agent (who had access to nuclear data from Los Alamos) reported to a different Soviet clandestine operator. But, in violation of the most commonsensical principles of compartmentation, this other agent also acted occasionally as a courier to transmit information from yet another Rosenberg agent to the other Soviet clandestine operator. When the other agent was caught, he was able to identify the other Rosenberg agent who in turn allowed the American counterintelligence opposition to further identify and then dismantle the Rosenberg network

The Sorge network in Japan also came a cropper from similar flaws of compartmentation thereby allowing the local counterintelligence opposition to dismantle the ring. The Sorge operation had two fatal flaws. The first fatal flaw was that Sorge and his sponsoring clandestine organization in Moscow underestimated the professional opposition, which in this case were the German and Japanese intelligence services. Sorge's compelling and ingratiating personality, and his analytical brilliance might have endeared him to key German officials in Tokyo and served to gain their trust, but it was sheer madness to assume that German counterintelligence people would not pick up on him and begin to scrutinize him in depth. Furthermore, when one of his Japanese agents became a confidant of the Japanese Prime Minister, it was also sheer madness to assume that Japanese counterintelligence would not notice it and probe the matter.

The second fatal flaw in Sorge's operation is that he functioned as both a clandestine operator who ran a series of agents, and as a secret agent himself. There was no non-descript, well-concealed, and well-buried supervisory clandestine operator in the equation, perhaps one who might have been under cover with diplomatic immunity in an embassy. Such an operator might have managed Sorge as an agent and also managed other elements of the ring, keeping them compartmented and acting as a cutout in implementing radio communications with the Soviet clandestine organization back home. In this case, open, flamboyant, high-profile Sorge did it all, and Sorge knew it all. So, when the first fatal flaw led to Sorge's compromise, he compromised everything.

Of course, as mentioned earlier, it is impossible to run clandestine operations with perfect operational security, with perfect cover, perfect concealment, and perfect compartmentation. An experienced operator must choose the ideal point where security and efficiency are most productively balanced. Still, all imperfections constitute opportunities for the counterintelligence opposition to exploit. So, it behooves all clandestine operators to work hard to keep those imperfections to a minimum despite the time-consuming and laborious exigencies of good clandestine tradecraft.

Damage Reports

Any clandestine operating service will from time to time suffer operational compromises. Of course, good operational security and hard-nosed counterintelligence scrutiny will go a long way to minimize any damage resulting from such compromises. But when a compromise does occur, the clandestine organization <u>must</u> assess the damage.

Its own counterintelligence personnel must review all past reporting in excruciating detail. The purpose is four-fold: 1) to determine if one's own service (and by extension its customer) has been deliberately fed false and misleading information, 2) to determine if any information that the clandestine operator revealed to the agent may have indicated to the other side the informational requirements of one's own service and of one's customer, 3) to pin-point errors in operational security and counterintelligence awareness on one's own side that led to the compromise, and 4) to determine how much overall compromise has occurred to the clandestine organization's assets, methodology, and personnel.

The foregoing are basic reasons behind the principle that clandestine operators must report all their clandestine activities, and that such reports must refer to aspects of operational security pertinent to the activities. But there are other reasons as well. For example, reporting formats (such as those described earlier in this book) generate checklists that reinforce thoroughness and establish patterns of thought that are essential for professionalism in espionage.

Another reason for extensive and systematic reporting is that it allows for review and tutelage of younger personnel in a profession where good security practices often prevent a superior from being physically present to look over a subordinate's shoulder.

A damage report is usually very long because it requires an in-depth analysis of an operation throughout its whole history. The complexity of a damage report precludes reproducing an exemplar in this brief book.

CHAPTER VIII

Non-Personal Communication

If a clandestine operator judges that the security risk to a secret-agent operation is particularly high, he will often reduce his direct contact with his agent to a minimum. Instead, he will communicate with him by non-personal means. This is often the preferred practice in particularly hostile operational environments.

Some direct contact with an agent will probably always be necessary in order to discuss problems, administer training, provide personal guidance, and to assess any counterintelligence aspects. But in many cases, the clandestine operator might radically reduce direct contact, or else carry out face-to-face contact on occasions when the agent is travelling outside his own country.

In all cases of non-personal communication, the clandestine operator must fully train the agent beforehand in the primary and alternate methods for contact. Furthermore, he must ensure that the agent is well versed in the basic principles of factual reporting, such as separating fact from inference, specifying subsources, proper dating, and so forth. After all, with non-personal communication, it would be difficult if not impossible for the clandestine operator to question the agent and clarify badly-reported details. Furthermore, the agent must also be completely trustworthy since it will more difficult to scrutinize and assess him on a continuing basis for counterespionage anomalies.

A clandestine organization might employ a variety of non-personal communication methods with an agent. Some techniques might relate to the agent's communication to the clandestine operator; others from clandestine operator to agent, with alternate and re-contact plans as necessary. Some systems are mixed; that is, in most cases they employ non-personal methods supplemented by less frequent face-to-face meetings from time to time.

Dead Drops

A classic method in spy movies or described in spy novels is the **_dead drop_** by which the agent deposits his reports or other material in a secret hiding place for the clandestine operator to pick up later. In general, it is preferable most of the time not to use such a method in the other direction; that is, for the clandestine operator to leave material for the agent to pick up. There is a sound reason for this.

If the local counterespionage service has any suspicions, it is probably with reference to the clandestine operator who might be a foreigner. One would not want the operator, who would be the one more likely to be under scrutiny, to lead the counterespionage service to the hiding place thereby allowing the professional counterintelligence opposition to identify the agent who comes to retrieve the material. It is far less likely that the agent, buried as he is in local society, would be under scrutiny.

A dead drop is a lot more complicated than it appears in spy movies or in spy novels. It's not simply a matter of finding a place to hide something for somebody else to pick up. It's a lot tougher to find an adequate place than it might seem at first blush, and other elements come into play as well.

Let's assume that back in Degenera, HOPEWARS/1 has by now learned to write adequate information reports for HANDLEMAN. He can now produce reports in which he gives good sub-sourcing, separates fact from inference, gives dates accurately, and also includes separate operational data on how he got the information. He also learned to report security aspects of his work for HANDLEMAN, how to assess personalities whom he meets, and the importance of reporting any new access he may enjoy.

He is able to fold such written matter into a tight package that might contain copies or else film of classified Degeneran documents, or perhaps drawings that are of informational or operational interest. He must now convey this small package to HANDLEMAN by putting it in a hiding place so HANDLEMAN can retrieve it without having to come into contact with HOPEWARS/1 directly.

The hiding place must be situated so that both parties can retrieve it without calling attention to themselves for being in the area. We don't, for example, want a senior government official going to a seedy part of town to load a drop near or around a strip club. The area where the drop is located, as well as the proximate place where it is situated, must be where both HANDLEMAN and HOPEWARS/1 can go without arousing suspicion or even attention.

After HOPEWARS/1 loads the drop, it must not remain loaded with material for too long. Murphy's Law ("If something can go wrong it will") dictates that sooner rather than later someone will stumble on it, and, if he reports it to the professional opposition, the subsequent investigation might eventually uncover the source. So, HOPEWARS/1 must be able to signal HANDLEMAN when the drop is loaded, and HANDLEMAN must then unload it as soon as possible.

In return, HANDLEMAN must be able to signal HOPEWARS/1 when he has unloaded the drop. If, for some reason he does not unload the drop, and HOPEWARS/1 does not get an unload signal, HOPEWARS/1 must then try to unload it himself to get his material back. It simply won't do to leave, say, the Degeneran war plans festering unattended somewhere, where sooner or later someone is bound to stumble upon the material.

Let's say the hiding place is on a ledge under the sink in the men's room in a large supermarket where HOPEWARS/1 and HANDLEMAN both go sometimes to buy groceries at a preset time, perhaps even accompanied by their wives. In such a scenario, HANDLEMAN and HOPEWARS/1 might be visible to each other at a distance,

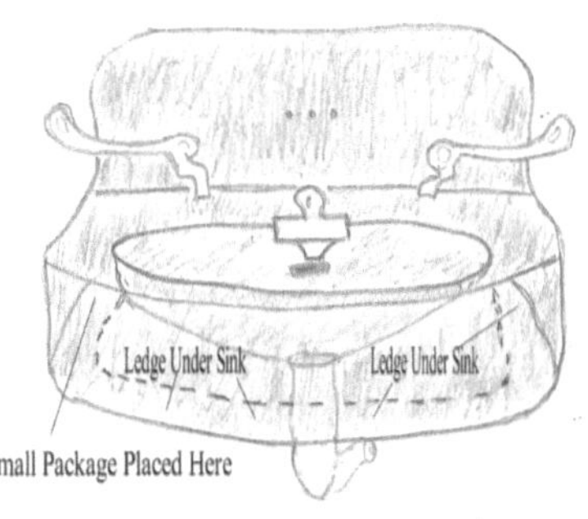

Note 1: Ledge is 10 cm wide

Note 2: Ceramic apron around sink hides underside from view

so when HOPEWARS/1 comes back from the men's room after hiding his material on the ledge, he removes his jacket which thereby signals HANDLEMAN, who is also in the supermarket, that the drop is loaded. After a short interval, HANDLEMAN meanders to the men's room and unloads the drop. Then he puts a white handkerchief in his breast pocket to signal that he has done so.

Such a dead drop in which the loader and unloader are visible to each other and can therefore signal each other directly is known as a "controlled drop," and it has the advantage that both participants can ensure that the drop remains loaded for the shortest possible time. HANDLEMAN made a rough sketch when he first identified the possible drop site.

Another Dead Drop

Not all dead drops need to be "controlled drops" that are loaded for only short periods. Even though we always want the drop to hold its materials for as short a time as possible, we can live with dead drops that can last for slightly longer periods.

Some dead drops, if situated in a less-frequented area, can remain loaded for longer periods and don't require the loader and unloader to be in the same area at the same time. Furthermore, signals can be in separate areas as well. There might be a chalk mark on a telephone pole that HANDLEMAN walks by every day. Or a flower pot placed on HOPEWARS/1's balcony, visible from the street along HANDLEMAN's daily route. And HANDLEMAN might establish a similar unload signal for HOPEWARS/1 to discern.

In any case, the loader and unloader <u>must</u> have some easy and evident cover reason for going to the drop site. Also, there <u>must</u> be effective concealment when loading or unloading the drop, and there <u>must</u> be effective cover and concealment for being at the signal sites and executing the signal.

Another example of a dead drop might be under a rock or in the hollow of a tree in a secluded part of a park where HOPEWARS1 occasionally goes for a run, and where HANDLEMAN can go as well for the same purpose without arousing suspicion. The time and date will be pre-set, preferably on a weekend relatively early in the morning when neither HANDLEMAN nor

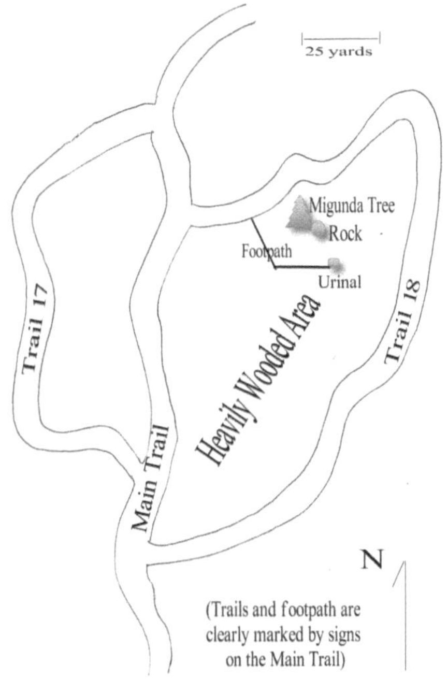

HOPEWARS/1 have to be at work. During his run in the park, HOPEWARS/1 will stop and visit a public urinal off of a certain trail a few yards from a certain tree which is hidden from view from the trail by a copse of other trees. After ensuring that nobody is in sight, he will lift a four-pound rock near the base of the tree and leave the package in a hole under it. Then he will resume his jog and go home. Once home he will move a flower pot on his balcony to a different location as signal that the drop is loaded. HANDLEMAN will see the balcony from his own apartment which is within sight. When he sees the load signal he will go to the Park, also as a jogger, visit the urinal, and unload the drop. Upon returning home, he will draw the blinds on his bedroom window as an unload signal visible from HOPEWARS/1's apartment. If HANDLEMAN does not or cannot unload the drop by a pre-arranged time, say late morning, HOPEWARS/1 will return to the site and unload the drop himself under cover of another jog later in the day.

There is no limit to the imagination that one might employ to set up a dead drop provided one incorporates as much as possible the principles of cover, concealment, and compartmentation to protect the drop from the notice of the public, of law enforcement, and of the professional opposition.

The Brush Pass

The **brush pass** is a classic technique used in many different forms to minimize the possibility that professional scrutiny might uncover a relationship between a secret agent and a clandestine operator. It does allow contact between the secret agent and his clandestine operator, but it is very brief and concealed.

The way NOT to carry out a brush pass is the way it is often depicted in movies or on TV. One sees the agent sitting on a park bench and then the clandestine operator comes and sits briefly on the same bench. Each is carrying a briefcase or a package or a folded newspaper. Then one gets up to leave and picks up the other person's briefcase, package or newspaper containing the envelope or other material to be passed. Thus, voila, they consummate the pass.

The foregoing is so dumb for reasons that anyone who has read this book so far should grasp. The cover (two people relaxing on a park bench) might not arouse the suspicion of the public who see them sitting together. And perhaps it might not catch the attention of any cop or other law-enforcement official whose antennae are out primarily for people who are obviously breaking the law. But it certainly would <u>not</u> fool the professional counterintelligence opposition which might be scrutinizing one or the other participant, and will want to know the identity of the person sitting on the same bench with the other one. More importantly, there is no concealment. In brush passes, concealment of the two people when they come together is more important than cover (even though both participants should still have cover stories for being where they are).

Indeed, concealment and brevity are the key factors in a brush pass. As long as one keeps that in mind, the brush pass offers considerable versatility. It is basically a quick handoff from one person to another. It can be done in a crowd where other people unwittingly shield the action. It can be done in a restaurant or night club or sporting event or department store or mall where one of the participants passes the other. It can be a hand-to-hand transfer, or the item being passed can be dropped into a shopping bag that the other is carrying. It can be done not only on the street, but in a store, at a social event, at picnic grounds, at the zoo, at a tourist venue, even at a diplomatic reception or other official diplomatic gathering.

But still, normal precautions should apply. In addition to the element of concealment, each participant must have a cover reason for being in the area such as shopping, going to a restaurant, or recreation, and the reason must be apparent to the casual observer, to law enforcement authorities, and be plausible to the professional opposition if either participant is questioned. Both participants should travel a counter-surveillance route before the brush pass. And in all cases, the recipient of the material should display a safety signal before material is passed to him.

Although a brush pass can be done in a crowded area, it is often better to go around a sudden corner to do it, or down a short corridor, or through some other relatively concealed spot where, for a brief moment or so, one will be out of sight if there happens to be surveillance behind either one.

Here is an example of a brush pass between HANDLEMAN and HOPEWARS/1 which might take place downtown in the capital city of Degenera: HOPEWARS/1 would go to the top of a subway stairwell at a precise pre-arranged time carrying a shopping bag with some purchases in it. Before descending to the subway, he will spend about two minutes

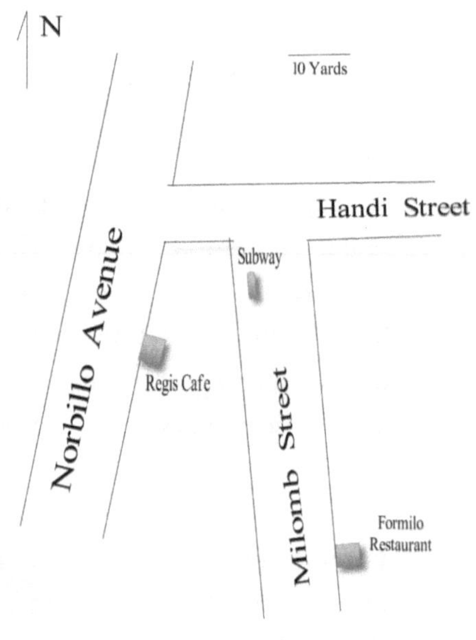

looking at the public notices posted on the street at the top of the subway stairs. Meanwhile, HANDLEMAN will be situated around a double corner (see sketch below) at the Regis café on Norbillo Avenue. The location is about a 20-second walk around one corner and then around another very near corner to the spot where HOPEWARS/1 will be standing reading the public notices. HANDLEMAN will have previously ordered a beverage at the Café' and will have paid for it immediately so he can leave at the right moment. He will then sit there for a while to drink it. At precisely the time that HOPEWARS/1 arrives at the top of the subway stairwell, HANDLEMAN will finish his drink, leave the café, walk about fifteen yards and take a right at Handi Street, then take another right ten yards later on Milomb Street. He will continue about five yards to where HOPEWARS/1 will be standing and exhibiting a pre-arranged safety signal. Walking past HOPEWARS/1, HANDLEMAN will unobtrusively drop his material into HOPEWARS/1's shopping bag and continue down Milomb Street towards the Formilo Restaurant where he will be joined by his wife for dinner. Meanwhile HOPEWARS/1, upon receiving the package in his shopping bag, will immediately go down into the subway station, mingle with other commuters, and take the subway home.

One of the advantages of this procedure is that it would foil observation by any surveillance mounted on HANDLEMAN. As he turns the first corner, the surveillant in the first position behind him wouldn't be able to observe him, although a surveillant across the street would of course see him proceed along Handi Street but when HANDLEMAN almost immediately takes a second right down Milomb Street he will be briefly out of sight of all surveillants until one of them rounds the second corner as well. By then, HANDLEMAN would have made the pass and HOPEWARS/1 will have disappeared down the subway stairs mingling with the people waiting for the next train. The surveillance would discern only HANDLEMAN hurrying down Milomb Street to the restaurant to meet his wife.

A variant of the dead drop is the so-called "car toss." In a car-toss scenario, HOPEWARS/1 would drive his car along a lonely country road, and toss a package out of the window perhaps into adjacent woods at a pre-arranged time and a pre-arranged spot, perhaps around a curve to conceal the act from any vehicle behind him. HANDLEMAN would come along shortly afterwards and pick it up. Of course, HOPEWARS/1 would have a cover destination to justify his being on the road, and HANDLEMAN would also need a cover for being on the road, and/or being in the woods, perhaps stopping his car briefly to go into the woods to urinate, or else being in the woods on a camping trip with his family. The difficulty with respect to a car toss lies in signaling when the agent tossed the material, and when the clandestine operator picked it up. The time necessary to execute a signal usually requires that the material lie on the ground for too long, which makes agents and operators nervous. Some clandestine organizations use only unload (i.e. pick up) signals after the operator has retrieved the material, the absence of which would require the agent to return to retrieve it. But this too has obvious drawbacks with respect to cover and concealment.

Secret Writing, Microdots and Electronic Means

A method of non-personal communication in classical espionage is **secret writing**. That is, a nondescript letter or other written material which also contains a second text written with an invisible substance which the recipient can "develop" chemically and then read. Typically, the secret text is written at right angles to the open text so that the latter does not obscure the readability of the secret text.

In general, it is better for a secret agent to use secret writing to communicate with his clandestine operator, and not the other way around. Why? In order for the agent to receive such messages he must often be in possession of incriminating chemicals that sometimes have to be mixed together. and sometimes even specialized equipment to "develop" the secret writing. But in sending a message, the agent usually needs to have only a single chemical in his possession which can perhaps be disguised as a medicine pill. In some cases, the agent may have been instructed how to concoct the "developer" when needed.

As for sending secret writing, a common procedure is to give the agent a sheet of paper that is completely saturated with the chemical. Such a piece of paper can serve as a "carbon" for writing the message. After writing the open cover letter, and turning the sheet at a right angle, the agent then places the "carbon" over it, and in turn places a blank sheet of paper over the carbon. Then he writes his secret message on the piece of paper, being careful to press lightly lest he make an impression on the paper that carries the cover letter. The message will transfer invisibly to the sheet containing the cover letter, after which the agent can destroy the top sheet of paper on which he wrote his secret message. He can conceal the carbon easily since it looks just like an ordinary piece of paper.

In addition, the cover text should contain a pre-arranged word or phrase as a signal that the letter contains secret writing and another word or phrase to serve as a safety signal to indicate that the letter was not written under duress.

Microdots, like secret writing, rely on a mail service. A microdot consists of a highly miniaturized photograph of a message or other document that can be pasted unobtrusively in an innocent letter or envelope (perhaps underneath the postage stamp) or in a book. Sometimes they are small enough to fit under a written period or other punctuation mark in the cover text, which is why they are called microdots. Since the preparation of a microdot requires considerable skill and sophisticated photographic equipment, they are typically used to convey messages from the clandestine organization to the secret agent. The agent need have only a strong magnifying lens, perhaps a jeweler's loupe, to read it. Of course, he must have a cover explanation for possessing such an item.

A detailed technical treatment of secret writing or microdots is beyond the scope of this book. Most clandestine operators and secret agents rely on the technical staff of their clandestine organizations for an appropriate system to use. There is also much public literature on the use of hidden texts, and the techniques continue to evolve. Totalitarian countries which closely scrutinize their mail, particularly international mail, use sophisticated techniques to check whether a letter might contain secret writing or a microdot. Clandestine organizations are constantly creating newer and better methods to foil such attempts.

Regardless of the scientific technicalities involved, the clandestine operator and his agent must still consider the basic principles of cover, concealment and compartmentation outlined at the beginning of this book, including safety signals. The outgoing microdot cover letter from the clandestine organization to the agent should be convincing and realistic, and should have a fictitious but convincing return address. And, as mentioned, it should also contain a key word or phrase to indicate that the letter contains a clandestine message, and also a safety signal to indicate that it is genuine.

The incoming microdot letter or secret writing letter might require another agent to function as an accommodation address to receive it and act as a go-between. He would later pass the letter to the secret agent recipient, perhaps by dead drop or brush pass. Such an intermediary, known as a *cutout*, might add somewhat to the secret agent's security, but would also weaken the compartmentation of the operation. This is a factor to be taken into consideration.

As a last point, it is important not to overuse an accommodation addresses either for sender or recipient. The best practice dictates that an accommodation address, like a safehouse, be used for one and only one secret agent.

Old Fashioned Radio

Another classical means of communication is radio. This can be ideal for an agent to receive messages from his clandestine organization, but it requires the agent to possess a simple short-wave radio set to do so.

Such messages might be a series of numbers read off by a human voice which the agent can decode with a code-pad given to him earlier, either directly by his clandestine operator or, for example, passed to him through a dead drop or brush pass. The procedure would, however, require him to possess code pads, and their possession would be incriminating. Such material would have to be well-concealed. To use a radio in reverse, that is to enable the agent to communicate to the clandestine organization, the agent must possess a transmitter, be proficient in its use, and he must have a very convincing cover for possessing it. He too might encode a message and broadcast it as a series of numbers.

Note, however, that authoritarian and totalitarian states monitor their airwaves closely and can pinpoint a transmitter by taking several readings from different positions. They can note the direction of broadcast, and then use triangulation to locate it. For that reason, an outgoing coded message is usually recorded and transmitted in a quick burst so as not to provide enough time to locate it.

Today, computers, laptops, and smart phones, can offer various methods to embed coded messages into e-mail or other electronic correspondence. Still, secret agents and clandestine operators must continue to apply the principles of cover, concealment and compartmentation to protect the fact, significance, and identity of the participants from the public, from law enforcement, and from the professional opposition.

Communication Plan for Use with Each Secret Agent

Sources of information in the form of controlled agents are the stock-in-trade of any clandestine organization. Their value lies not only in monitoring ongoing events behind the scenes, but particularly in reporting such information to their clandestine operators during fast-moving situations and crises.

For that reason, it is essential for a clandestine organization to enjoy constantly <u>reliable</u> and <u>secure</u> contact with its agents even in difficult and dangerous operating environments. Fortunately, if the reader has paid attention to this book so far, he'll understand that a clandestine organization, through its professional clandestine operators, has at its disposal a plethora of techniques to ensure the constant viability of such contacts. These techniques, as described above with examples, range from regular personal meetings, alternate meetings, emergency non-scheduled meetings, recontact meetings between an agent and a new clandestine operator, as well as a variety of non-personal techniques, and if necessary the use of technical aids (next chapter). They are all designed to protect the fact and significance of the contact and identities of the participants from the public, law enforcement, and professional oppositions by means of cover, concealment, and compartmentation.

The degree to which a clandestine operator and his agent make use of the foregoing techniques will depend on the ability and willingness of the agent to absorb all that is necessary to implement them, on the requisites of the environment, and on the experienced judgment of the operator. Ultimately each agent should have a full communication plan tailored to his abilities and to his operating environment. The operative word here is "tailored."

HOPEWARS/1, although motivated by profit and perhaps by some ego gratification, might not yet be ready or willing to carry out overly cumbersome maneuvers to communicate with HANDLEMAN - maneuvers that would underscore the dangers of his activity, maneuvers that appear risky, and maneuvers that are probably not necessary given the relatively easy operating environment in Degenera. But it is HANDLEMAN's job to pull HOPEWARS/1 more tightly into the fold, and eventually have him accept his role as a fully-trained professional spy against the day that he might have to operate as such if the operating environment worsens. If the government of Degenera were to become more and more authoritarian, and if the counterintelligence services were to become more and more sophisticated, HANDLEMAN's clandestine organization would want its contact with HOPEWARS/1 to rely less and less on face-to-face meetings within Degenera, and instead rely more and more frequently on other means.

CHAPTER IX

Technical Support

Obviously, the use of such techniques as secret writing, microdots, and radio requires that any clandestine organization be able to provide technical support to human-source collection and covert action operations.

Equipment and gadgets for supporting clandestine operations seem to hold an endless fascination for spy-buffs and for the general public. But the professional clandestine operator who adheres to the mantra of cover, concealment, and compartmentation knows that it is extraordinarily difficult to devise a cover for possessing many types of spy gear. Cover for the possession of such equipment is not likely to fool even the public opposition, much less the law enforcement opposition or the professional counterintelligence opposition. The primary requirement for the protection of spy gear is, therefore, concealment.

After all, unless your status cover in a given country is that of a theater performer how do you justify having wigs, false beards, masks or other disguise material in your possession? Unless your cover is that of professional photographer, how do you justify possessing sophisticated gear for making or reading microdots? Even so, how can you explain that miniature camera in your packet of cigarettes or in your wristwatch? Unless your cover is that of a chemist, how do you explain possession of chemicals to write or read secret writing? Unless your cover involves electronics, how do you explain that sophisticated radio transceiver of yours, or that simple short-wave receiver in a country where the government forbids residents from owning them? Unless you are a locksmith, why would you have lock-picking tools? And what plausible explanation can you come up with to explain a secret compartment in your furniture, briefcase, pen, or shoes? How about codes used to decipher or encipher incoming or outgoing messages? What plausible cover story can you give for having such material? What possible reason can an innocent businessman, office worker, or writer give for possessing various packets of false identity documents?

Spy gear not only does not lend itself well to convincing cover stories, but it also introduces unwelcome variables to an operation. It adds to the number of things that can go wrong in a world where Murphy's Law can lead to disaster. Therefore, all good clandestine operators and good secret agents should resist using spy gear unless it is absolutely necessary. They should employ such gear only when the advantages far outweigh the risks. But, despite the disadvantages of spy gear in terms of plausible cover for possessing it, there are indeed times when circumstances justify it. Weighing the risks of possessing and using spy gear is one more important judgment call that clandestine operators must make.

Disguises

A disguise can be useful to a clandestine operator if upon engaging in a given activity he does not wish to be remembered or identified later. On the flip side, the operator has to consider the hassle it entails, the need for additional time and a concealed venue for donning the disguise, plus the need for fake documentation in case he is questioned while wearing it, not to mention the difficulty, if not impossibility, of citing a cover if it is discovered. On balance, a clandestine operator would probably not need to use a disguise when handling a trusted agent (especially if the agent does not know his operator's true name or status cover within the country). But he might don a disguise if he is going to hang around a particular area to case it for, say, a surreptitious entry, or go to a strange place to unload a dead drop, or perhaps go to some installation where he would not normally go and where he might attract attention.

A particular situation when a disguise might be in order is when a clandestine operator handles a secret agent under what in espionage parlance is called a ***false flag***. It means that the agent was recruited under false pretenses as to which clandestine service is really sponsoring the relationship and which country is its real customer. Such a case would be a secret agent in the Republic of Remotia who is devoted to Communist China, who thinks he is working for a Chinese clandestine organization, and wants Remotia to be in the Chinese camp. The clandestine operator would be an ethnic Chinese person decked out in a disguise so that the secret agent is far less likely at any point to discern his real nationality or real sponsoring country, or be able to describe him meaningfully later.

Another situation is when a clandestine organization has some lingering counterintelligence doubts about an agent, and wants to ensure that he not be able to describe or identify the clandestine operator who is handling him, For example, if HANDLEMAN'S organization has some misgivings about HOPEWARS/1, then when HANDLEMAN's tour is over he night introduce HOPEWARS/1 to a new clandestine operator who would handle HOPEWARS/1 in alias and disguise.

One of the advantages of such an anonymous relationship is that if the clandestine organization finally does come to believe that the secret agent has been turned against it and is now a double agent working for the professional opposition, it need not go through an elaborate termination procedure with parting gifts, expressions of esteem, and so forth. It need only to stop showing up for meetings. In such a case, the secret agent would not know whom to contact to revive the relationship, or whom to point to.

A good disguise is more than a false beard or a wig. It must be crafted so as to distort the salient and memorable aspects of a person's body and face. If, say, clandestine operator Joe Smith is a neatly combed, brown-haired, well-dressed man of medium height with distinctive blue eyes, then putting a beard on him would be of little use. He would become merely the same old Joe Smith but with a beard. Instead, if he wears elevator shoes, a black wig with pomade, heavy horn-rimmed tinted glasses, and a cheap foreign suit, he is far less likely to be associated later with his true appearance. Other refinements are orthotics in the shoes to alter one's gait, and even devices to put in the mouth to mask one's speech.

The use of disguises for agent meetings often calls for a safehouse. You don't want to be seen walking out of your own house or apartment building sporting a disguise, because people in your neighborhood who are familiar with you (such as your janitor) might still recognize you, or if they don't recognize you, question you as to what you are doing in that building. Instead, the clandestine operator goes to a safehouse; ideally an apartment in a low-scale part of town in an unfrequented neighborhood. The building preferably would have more than one exit. There the clandestine operator would don his disguise and leave by another exit, and return later to change back.

Other uses of disguises do not necessarily involve a clandestine operator's regular contact with a secret agent. Sometimes an operator or an agent uses his disguise only on a one or two-time basis. For example, we might use a native Degeneran support agent, who of course speaks the local language and fits well into local society, to rent a small apartment as a safehouse for HANDLEMAN and HOPEWARS/1. But if the support agent does many other different tasks for us, we might want to hide his identity lest the compromise of the safehouse lead the professional opposition to identify him, which in turn could lead them to any other work he does in our behalf. So, when he rents the safehouse we put him in disguise. In this way, if the safehouse is compromised, he won't be physically identified later. He would pay the rent by anonymous means, say by mailing a check from a bank account that was similarly created in disguise, and whose balance we replenish by mail. Of course, renting the safehouse and opening an account will require false documentation. In fact, any time one uses a disguise one should have false documents to go with it. Documentation is also a technical support function.

Documentation

A truly professional clandestine organization must be capable of creating or acquiring all kinds of false documents. But most such documentation must go one step beyond mere creation or acquisition. In order to protect the bearer, such documentation must be "backstopped" so if anyone checks with the entity that ostensibly issued the documentation to the bearer, there will be a record indicating that the documentation is bona fide.

Backstopping usually requires either the cooperation of the issuing office or else a secret agent who works there. So, if you are traveling to the Kingdom of Eyesore ostensibly as a Livonian citizen, there had better be a record of your passport with the Livonian passport authorities and a record of your driver's license in the motor vehicle office back in Livonia, Backstopping is particularly necessary when the documentation is to be used in an interface with foreign authorities.

And, of course, the user of such documentation had better have a plausible cover story for whatever he is doing when using it. But it is difficult to concoct a cover story for a person operating under a given identity for possessing other counterfeit material in another identity. That is why it is best for someone doing very risky work to possess only one such set of documents. Varied documentary material is best kept by a clandestine operator who might be in a less sensitive position. Even so, if the clandestine operator keeps such material in his home or office for distribution to different agents when necessary, it might still be vulnerable to the scrutiny of servants, service providers, burglars, or even surreptitious entries by the local professional opposition.

Indeed, the possession of documentation that is shown to be false (or even worse, different sets of documents for which there can be no satisfactory explanation), is deeply incriminating, just like the possession of disguise material. So rather than rely on a good cover for possessing it, one must rely primarily on concealment to protect it. Here too, technical support can help.

Concealment Devices

The technical support personnel of a good clandestine organization can build hiding places into the structure of one's home, into furniture, into objects one has around the house, and into things one carries. Such secret compartments can range from the very simple to the extremely sophisticated.

There is no limit to the imagination when creating concealment devices. They can be under stairs, in baseboards, in walls behind shelves, in stairwell railings, in door jambs, in electrical systems, in furniture, in real or fake plumbing fixtures, in posts and beams, in window sills, behind false walls, in closets, in briefcases, cigarette lighters, pens, suitcases, eyeglass cases, belts, shoes and other articles of clothing, computers, and smart-phones.

One must, however, remember two things about such concealment devices. First, their discovery by the opposition (like the discovery of their contents) is usually a security disaster even if they contain no incriminating material at the moment of discovery. The very possession of such a device is indicative of clandestine activity. Second, if the opposition believes a certain object contains a concealment device, there is nothing to stop them from finding it upon detailed close inspection.

For the foregoing reasons, a clandestine operator or a secret agent should use concealment devices primarily to prevent casual observation of the material stored in it, or to withstand routine scrutiny as in customs inspection at the border. For example, if a secret agent has made copies of classified documents in his office, it would be a good idea for him to store them in a concealment device in his home until he can pass them to his clandestine operator. When bringing such documents to a meeting with his clandestine operator, it might be wise to carry them in a secret compartment in a portfolio or briefcase. Ditto for the clandestine operator with sensitive material in his possession. Such devices would protect the material in case of an accident or other untoward event.

It should be obvious that different levels of sophistication are often necessary when using concealment devices. It is one thing to keep sensitive material in a secret compartment in a bookcase or desk so it won't come to the casual attention of others in the household. It is quite another to smuggle such material through a customs inspection at a border crossing where law enforcement is on the lookout for contraband or security-relevant material.

Again, one must weigh the security advantage of a concealment device against the risk of having it in one's possession which, if discovered, would be prima facie evidence of clandestine intent.

Flaps and Seals

The art of surreptitiously opening the flaps of envelopes and the seals on written messages is an ancient one. In classical espionage, intelligence services maintained skilled craftsmen who could remove and later re-apply (or duplicate) wax seals.

Today the challenge is sealed envelopes. The art can range from steaming open a letter or treating it chemically to remove the glue, to simply tearing open an envelope and, after examining the contents, replacing it with a duplicate envelope bearing the correct postage stamp, forged cancellation marks, and forged address, and sending it on its way.

Some mail intercept operations can be very useful in acquiring background information on an individual in order to assess his or her susceptibilities and vulnerabilities, or else to uncover counterintelligence leads. Often such an operation requires a secret agent who works in the post office who can turn over to his clandestine operator a target's mail for scrutiny.

It should be noted that the art of "flaps and seals" works both ways. A professional counterintelligence service operating with official authority in its own country can easily scrutinize mail moving through its country's postal channels. Such scrutiny can not only uncover susceptibility and vulnerability information on the writer or recipient, but also allow the scanning of suspicious mail for secret writing or microdots. As the scanning techniques of the professional opposition become more sophisticated (ultra violet illumination, microscopic survey of paper fibers, the use of chemical markers, and so forth), the clandestine organization's concealment techniques must improve commensurably.

Telephone Taps and Microphones

Let us say that a clandestine organization wants to tap a telephone or install a listening device in a building in a foreign country where the clandestine organization has no legal status and no legal control over the environment. In such a situation, one can't go to the telephone company's central office, flash a badge, and get access to the transmission wires coming from a target phone. Nor can one go to the superintendent of an apartment building and legally require him to provide access to a given apartment. For that reason, such operations in foreign countries have to be more complicated and sophisticated.

For clandestine telephone taps abroad, it would help to have a local telephone employee on the payroll as a secret agent. He would be a person who has authority and cover to access telephone junction boxes or the telephone wiring inside an apartment building or at other points on the telephone circuits in any given neighborhood. One might think that all that the agent has to do would be to cross-connect a target's telephone wires with another telephone line leading to the place where one would listen to or record the telephone conversations. But there is danger in such a procedure.

If the cross connection is discovered, it would lead directly to those who are listening in on the conversations or who service the recordings. So, the technical support staff has to devise methods to conceal any cross connection. Also, instead of allowing the cross-connected wires to lead to the listeners, they might lead to a small transmitter embedded in the walls of a building or elsewhere in the neighborhood circuity. A listening post would of course be somewhere within range of the transmitter, but the range can be extensive enough to protect the listening post, and reach as far as another building.

Another danger is that the transmissions might be picked up by anyone nearby who uses a radio with wide-range frequency reception, who realizes that someone is monitoring someone's telephone somewhere, and decides to call the authorities. For that reason, it would be advantageous for the transmission signal to be relatively weak, and perhaps electronically coded and thus disguised. Ideally, the telephone linesman himself could be in disguise with false identification and false license plates on his truck, so that he would not be accurately remembered later if there were a compromise.

All of the foregoing requires technical support. We are talking about sophisticated technical support by technicians versed in the principles of clandestinity and operational security, who understand the uses of cover, concealment and compartmentation to protect a clandestine activity, its significance, and its participants from the public opposition, from law enforcement, and from professional counterintelligence.

Bugging a room to monitor non-telephone conversations is quite a different matter. Sometimes, in the case of an apartment, it can be as easy as acquiring an apartment next door (under suitable cover, of course), drilling carefully through the wall, making a pinhole opening, and inserting a microphone. Sometimes a surreptitious entry to a target apartment is necessary in order to plant a microphone/transmitter that will transmit whatever it picks up. Such entry operations have their own set of protocols to ensure cover, concealment, and compartmentation.

The building has to be cased thoroughly, and there must be adequate cover for the caser himself to be outside and sometimes inside the building to perform the casing adequately. The clandestine operator must learn the movements of the residents, must identify a means of access to the premises, and chart out escape routes if the entry operation goes sour. The clandestine operator has to arrange to put the residents under surveillance during the entry in order to give warning if they suddenly decide to return while the entry is in progress. As little as possible should be disturbed during the entry, and an instant photo should be taken at the outset to ensure that at the end everything is left as it was. And, of course the transmitter must be well concealed and it should transmit a masked and coded signal that would not likely attract attention or be identified accidently. One should also note that transmitters are especially susceptible to electronic anti-bugging sweeps which, if carried out, would detect the signal, coded or not. For this reason, it is usually not wise to bug a place that is used by intelligence officers or top diplomats.

One must note that the bulk of the "take" from a telephone tap or a bugging operation is likely to be useless mundane stuff, so it is rarely cost-effective to listen in "live" to such conversations. There are many far-fetched Hollywood images of people secretly listening in to telephone conversations; perhaps a telephone linesman perched up on a pole who is up there precisely at the moment that a meaningful conversation is taking place. So is the scenario of some well-paid guys manning a listening post around the clock. Rather, the clandestine organization should record the "take" electronically, after which support personnel would transcribe it for later scrutiny by clandestine operators.

Buried in the "take" might be useful operational information such as who is sleeping with whom, who is unhappy about not being promoted, who has a gripe about his/her boss, who is having financial problems, who is in any kind of trouble, who is going to be traveling, who has different tastes and interests, and so forth. It might also, on occasion, provide political or economic information worthy of dissemination as formal information reports. This might occur for example if you are listening in to a high official of a target entity who deals regularly with his subordinates by telephone, or if you bug a safehouse that another service uses for its agent meetings.

One of the dumber bugging scenarios got widespread publicity many years ago. It was the famous Martini Cocktail in which the olive was a microphone/transmitter, and the toothpick was the antenna. The Martini could be put close to two people talking at a diplomatic cocktail party. Sounds cool, doesn't it? Well it isn't. The chances of two people discussing something of value at that moment (when the Martini is nearby) is very low. And then there's the old listening post problem as to where you'll be stationed to listen to it.

Agent Communication

Agent communication is often the most vulnerable aspect of a clandestine organization's relationship with its secret agents. Technical support can be of great help. We have already cited secret writing and microdots, and then concealment devices can also be used when carrying incriminating material to and from a clandestine meeting, or to a dead drop or brush pass site.

Consider a clandestine operator who has excellent cover for status (that is, well embedded in the local environment) and is unlikely to be singled out for hostile scrutiny. Say he meets or communicates regularly and securely with his agents either by personal meetings, dead drops, or brush passes. But also suppose that it would be too dangerous for the clandestine operator himself to convey his own operational reports or the reports of his agents to his clandestine organization whose personnel are under secure diplomatic immunity in their country's embassy, but under intense scrutiny. In such a case, the organization might issue a short-range transmitter to a well-buried clandestine operator who is not under official cover and not likely to be under scrutiny. He, in turn, can use it to send his reports and operational correspondence by radio to his counterparts inside his country's embassy.

Such a transmitter should be capable of transmitting material in quick bursts, so as to minimize accidental discovery of the transmission and preclude the professional opposition from locating the source by directional analysis and triangulation. Sometimes the clandestine operator might be able to carry such a transmitter to different places near the embassy for transmission and thereby confound the opposition even further. Of course, the clandestine operator would need a concealment device for the transmitter, or else the device might be made to appear as an innocuous radio, in which case it can be hidden in plain sight under cover of its ostensible use.

And for reciprocal communication from the clandestine organization to the clandestine operator, it can be through enciphered coded messages broadcast over open short-wave channels which the operator can decipher with his codes, which of course he has to keep concealed. The clandestine organization, either through a courier agent or another clandestine operator under cover in his country's embassy, can pass such codes to the operator from time to time via dead drop or brush pass, but of course such activities would be kept to a minimum. The clandestine organization can supplement all this communication with occasional direct meetings if and when the clandestine operator makes a trip outside the country.

Operational Philosophy

In our modern times, technical support for human source operations is truly indispensable.

A good technical-support component of a clandestine organization should maintain many capabilities in addition to disguises, false documentation, concealment devices, communication hardware, and so forth. Technical support can, for example, miniaturize all kinds material to make it easier to conceal or pass by dead drop, or to use as listening devices or cameras. Some clandestine organizations use technical support to create weapons for assassination.

Another discipline that might fall under the rubric of technical support is graphological analysis to assess the character and personality of a recruitment prospect. Indeed, a technical support unit might employ psychologists on its staff to do the same. And of course, a technical support component must be able to create instruments of sabotage such as explosives or corrosive material, perhaps disguised as an innocuous powder such as flour or talcum.

Despite the foregoing, most experienced clandestine operators are deeply familiar with Murphy's Law and have a deep instinct to "keep it simple." They would rightly try to avoid dependence on "spy gear" unless it provides a demonstrable advantage.

As we know, most experienced clandestine operators are very sensitive to threat from various opposition forces such as the public, law enforcement and professional counterintelligence services. These threats, to one degree or another, pervade all operational environments, and their existence engenders in the clandestine operator a professional instinct to apply cover, concealment, and compartmentation as much as possible to all clandestine activity. The foregoing militates against the use of many technical support devices because they present additional variables and vulnerabilities which must be covered, concealed, and compartmented, and in most cases preclude any convincing cover story if discovered.

Yet, as some of the examples in this and previous chapters illustrate, there are times when spy gear is definitely useful, and the drawbacks far outweigh the risks. Any successful clandestine operator obviously <u>must</u> weigh carefully the advantage of technical support in any operation in terms of safety and efficiency against the inherent disadvantage to the principles of operational security.

Indeed, human source espionage is not an easy profession, and requires much judgment to minimize risk.

CHAPTER X

Types of Agents and Covert Action

Information Reporting Agents

We have already discussed the acquisition and management of information-reporting agents. These are secret agents who are so situated as to have natural access to non-public information of interest to a clandestine organization and its sponsor. The fictitious Samilo Dravunio Hembersol, described earlier in this book as a middle-level Air Force officer on the Degeneran General Staff, is an example of such an agent, and was encrypted HOPEWARS/1.

Such an agent is often referred to as "a penetration" (in this case a penetration of the Degeneran General Staff) or sometimes as an "agent in place." Acquiring and managing such reporting-agents is the ultimate job of a clandestine information-reporting organization. As I have elucidated, it is a difficult and risky undertaking.

It requires (among other things) a personality assessment of a potential agent, an understanding of his activities, his attitudes, his beliefs, his problems, his career, and his family. Many of these factors emerge during a covert background investigation. Other factors emerge during personal contact between the agent candidate and a clandestine operator, or between the agent candidate and already-recruited agent spotters.

The acquisition of information-reporting agents requires an un-squeamish willingness to exploit information about them, not only to consummate a recruitment, but also to continue binding the agent to the clandestine organization as a trustworthy subordinate.

After we recruit a secret agent, we can improve the security of the relationship between him and his clandestine operator by the judicious management of our resources according to the principles of operational security outlined in this book.

But there are times when an information-reporting agent morphs into something else.

Covert Action Agents

Let us say that over the years, our agent, HOPEWARS/1, serves his clandestine organization well as a penetration of the Degeneran Air Force and General Staff. Thanks to him, the clandestine organization's sponsoring government knows everything there is to know about the Degeneran military establishment.

Furthermore, HOPEWARS/1 has also been a valuable source on Degeneran political and economic matters since members of his family are long-time loyalists of Degenera's ruling People's

Democratic Party (PDP), and HOPEWARS/1's wife is herself a member of a very prominent and rich Degeneran family.

These connections have also helped HOPEWARS/1 rise to high rank in the Degeneran military hierarchy, especially since, at the behest of his clandestine operators, HOPEWARS/1 has dissembled his aversion to the PDP and, instead, presented himself as an ardent supporter

Then one day, it occurs to the clandestine organization's customer (even if the customer does not know HOPEWARS/1's identity) that, given the excellent intelligence reporting on high-level Degeneran military matters, the organization must have one or several very well-placed high-level sources who possibly could, at the direction of the clandestine organization, influence the course of events in Degenera to support the interests of the customer country. In such a case he would become a covert action agent as well as an information-reporting agent.

But a number of dilemmas present themselves as HOPEWARS/1 rises in rank and influence. Of course when HOPEWARS/1 reaches a high position, he will continue to supply his clandestine operator with trustworthy information, but at the same time it becomes more and more difficult for the clandestine organization to communicate with him covertly. If HOPEWARS/1 eventually rises to the highest positions, and has an entourage around him, it might become problematic to carry out any concealed contact. In such a case, the security of his relationship with the clandestine organization would hinge less and less on concealment and more and more on excellent cover to justify meetings with ostensibly legitimate contacts.

Furthermore, let's assume that if HOPEWARS/1 were to become more than merely an information source, and instead were to morph into a proponent and implementer of policies that redound to the sponsor's interest, he might then become suspect to his own people which would eventually erode his position of authority and access. Therefore, the sponsoring organization must handle and guide him with particular care.

But not all covert-action agents need to be highly placed in order to act on behalf of the customers of a clandestine organization. For example, a clandestine organization might have some journalists as secret agents on its payroll to plant stories that influence public attitudes. Although journalism is an obvious area wherein a clandestine organization might run an agent, there is no limit as to other areas where a clandestine organization might recruit secret agents to influence the course of events in another country. In one country where astrology was the rage, a clandestine organization had a secret agent who wrote an astrology column in the paper!!

Agents of Influence

An ***agent of influence*** is technically a covert action agent but with a difference. Perhaps he should not even be designated an "agent." The phrase "agent of influence" designates a person who does <u>not</u> have the classic and disciplined employee-employer relationship with any clandestine operators, but through his relationship with them, they can still count on him to support a clandestine organization's customer.

Consider the stages of agent acquisition outlined In Chapter II of this book. Assume that one or more clandestine operators may have established close personal relationships with HOPEWARS/1, done favors for each other, and acquired knowledge of HOPEWARS/1's susceptibilities and vulnerabilities as described in that chapter. Then assume that, for one reason or another, the clandestine organization decides against "popping the question" and does not make a formal recruitment proposal to HOPEWARS/1. Instead, clandestine operators maintain friendly and mutually-beneficial contact with him over the years. Then, at some point in the future, when HOPEWARS/1 rises in power and influence, the clandestine operators, along with their clandestine organization and its customer government, find that they have a Friend in high places in Degenera whom they might count on to act favorably towards them.

And _that_ is an "agent of influence," although from the counterintelligence and legal perspectives it is probably inaccurate to consider such person an "agent." Such a relationship is difficult to prove or to criminalize since there is no employee-employer relationship, and often not even a communication channel for the clandestine organization to issue any instructions.

The Russians are reputed to be very skillful in developing agents of influence. A foreign politician or businessman or labor leader or top bureaucrat, howsoever smart and shrewd he is in his own specialty, is often no match for a highly-trained and competent clandestine operator who is skilled at leading a target down the garden path into a deep relationship that is profitable to his organization and its customer.

This is particularly true if the target is youthful, inexperienced beyond his specialty, suffers from an inflated ego, or has a profound psychological need for recognition, a desire for adulation, and a need to "belong." The clandestine operators on the other side will certainly know how to exploit such traits.

Support Agents

Earlier in this book we referred to **support agents** who can enhance the techniques for acquiring and managing other agents who are reporters of information. Every overseas component of a clandestine organization should have a stable of support agents.

We have already mentioned the use of such agents to provide safehouses and accommodation addresses. Or spotter agents who, while themselves do not enjoy access to information of intelligence interest, can identify people who might enjoy such access and might be susceptible to recruitment. Perhaps a personnel officer in a target organization might identify a potential penetration of that organization, or a professor at the university could identify young comers among the students who could have a bright career in the local environment and might be "recruitable." Such a spotter agent, while not having direct access to information of intelligence interest might have direct personal access to others who <u>do</u> have access to such information, and might be able to elicit such information for passage to his or her clandestine operator. We might obviously call such an agent an *access agent*, although the agent's information would of course be second-hand and therefore of less value than if reported directly from someone with first-hand access. The fabled Mata Hari was such a second-hand access agent because of her relationship with knowledgeable people on both sides during World War I.

Other support agents would be a number of local surveillants who could observe people and places where a clandestine operator might have difficulty venturing without attracting attention. There are many other kinds of support agents who can be of great value. How about an owner of a car-rental establishment who, under suitable cover, can make available vehicles that are not traceable to a clandestine operator nor associated with an information-reporting agent. Or how about the services of a local police officer who has access to police records that would enable a clandestine operator to check the background of a recruitment target or other person of interest. Or else, a legitimate private investigator recruited as a secret agent who could do much the same for a clandestine organization.

A clerk in the local motor vehicle department might be able to issue bogus drivers licenses to help a clandestine operator build a false identity for a secret agent. An agent situated in the Ministry of Foreign Affairs can issue passports and backstop them by creating related passport files in case anybody wants to check the legitimacy of the passport and its holder. Such a capability in one country can create identities for agents or clandestine operators who could then travel anywhere in the world, and therefore benefit a clandestine organization on a global scale.

Someone among the titled aristocracy of a traditional society could be of use in writing recommendations or giving entrée to clandestine operators or secret agents who are seeking access to certain sectors of society. A physician could make a useful support agent if you want a secret agent treated secretly for a disorder, or if you want a bogus medical diagnosis for your agent in order to get him transferred from an overseas assignment back to his home country where his usefulness would be much greater. The manager of a large luxury hotel can be of great use in providing temporary safehouses (in reality "saferooms") under bogus names, or else could keep an eye on specific guests who might be of interest to a clandestine operator. Also, the house detective in a large, major hotel would be an important asset because he could check up on guests, monitor their movements, note the comings and goings of visitors, and even provide discreet entry for planting listening devices.

And of course, an all-purpose agent at an airport or train station can be of great value in checking the movements of specific people, advising on security measures being taken by the local law-enforcement or professional opposition, and perhaps even providing tickets on short notice.

Last, in the chapter on counterintelligence, we already mentioned double agents who ostensibly work for one clandestine organization but are actually spying against their own organization at the behest of another organization. Such agents are sometimes referred to as "counterspies."

Cutouts

A very important type of support agent is known as a ***cutout***. A cutout is a mutually trusted intermediary, or a method or channel of communication that facilitates the exchange of information between agents. Or, in the context of clandestine relationships described in this book, a go-between who carries out the communication between a clandestine operator and his clandestine agent.

For example, in the case of HOPEWARS/1, the agent's clandestine operator HANDLEMAN might be under such close hostile scrutiny by the local counterintelligence opposition that he would find it expedient to employ a cutout agent, whom he can meet securely under superb cover and concealment, and who would be less likely to arouse the suspicion of the local authorities, to pass information to HOPEWARS/1 by means of a brush pass, or else to unload one of HOPEWARS/1's dead drops. Such a cutout, or go-between, would be particularly useful as a courier if HANDLEMAN resides in a different country and cannot travel to Degenera securely to contact HOPEWARS/1. And of course, such cutouts must have good cover for their movements.

Needless to say, the injection of an additional agent into such an operation decreases compartmentation. A judgment call is necessary as to whether the enhanced security resulting from placing HANDLEMAN one step away from a direct role in communicating with HOPEWARS/1 is worth using a cutout to communicate with him. The security of using a cutout is obviously enhanced if he does not know the identity of either the sender or receiver of the communication.

Loss of Compartmentation

Needless to say, when employing support agents in a clandestine operation, a clandestine operator must weigh their usefulness against the disadvantage of weakened compartmentation which always occurs when more and more people become aware of an operation. But there are ways to minimize the risk. For example (as mentioned earlier) it is a bad idea to use a safehouse (and by extension the safehouse keeper) for more than one operation. Ditto for using a cutout to service more than one agent.

We have iterated that in cases when employing a support agent in a variety of tasks (such as surveillance, investigations, or backstopping the cover stories of others), it is always a good practice to bury the task among many other tasks, involving several people to be investigated, surveilled, backstopped, or documented, in order to lessen the possibility of the target being singled out too obviously. In the case of backstopping or documenting, the support agent can do it in a false name when the secret agent being backtopped or documented is operating in a false identity.

There is a second advantage when we impose many tasks on support agents beyond merely camouflaging a clandestine organization's specific interest. It helps to assess the performance of the support agents themselves, sharpen their skills, and accustom them to their service with the clandestine organization. But even when a support agent is kept busy on a variety of tasks, it is important that a clandestine operator always guard against the overuse of support agents against any specific target. This is true, for example, in the case of safehouse keepers or accommodation addresses. In these cases, it is probably better to change safehouses and accommodation addresses regularly rather than use them for too long, lest they attract undue attention.

The only guiding doctrine to apply to these situations is a proper balance of cover, concealment, and compartmentation to protect the fact, identities, and significance of an operation from the public, law-enforcement, and professional oppositions. These are the judgment calls that clandestine operators must make.

By the way, multi-tasking of agents to bury true operations among them, need not be solely for the purpose of minimizing risks stemming from weakened compartmentation. The injunction to "keep an agent busy" also applies to agents-in-place as information reporters. In addition to an agent's true information-collecting requirements, the clandestine organization should task such an agent to collect information that the clandestine organization already has in its possession from other sources. We have made this point before. Not only does it de-emphasize the clandestine organization's real focus if the operation is compromised; it also serves as an ongoing counterintelligence testing mechanism for assessing and reassessing the truthfulness, viability, and security of its agents. Agent testing must be an ongoing activity.

The Clandestine Operator as a Secret Agent

Earlier in this book I underscored the difference between a secret agent who operates in a place where his clandestine operator cannot go, and the clandestine operator himself who recruits the secret agent and handles him.

There are, however, times when it is useful to have a trained clandestine operator directly on the scene functioning as an agent himself. For example, in a country where members of the clandestine organization's country are looked upon with great suspicion, or where the clandestine organization's country has no relations with the target country, it might not be advisable for most clandestine operators to operate there as foreigners. In such a case, it might be possible for the clandestine organization to use one of its trained clandestine operators who can appear as having a different nationality (perhaps even a national of the target country) and function under some sort of status cover to report on local conditions and also handle subordinate agents.

In such a case, we may consider the clandestine operator to be simultaneously a secret agent. Putting such an agent in place can often be very tricky. He must pass convincingly as the national of the host country or a national of a third country. His cover for being in the country must be real and functional. He must be exceptionally well-trained. And of course, the clandestine organization must consider compartmentation issues stemming from the operator's knowledge of other agents, and his lack of his own diplomatic or other official protection if he comes under hostile scrutiny.

There is yet another kind of clandestine operator who also functions as an agent. He is known as a "sleeper." A clandestine organization that is patient and well-funded may insert a thoroughly trained and trustworthy person into a target country, keep him there for many years to live and work while posing as a native or an immigrant, and let him build a life for himself and his family. In that way, he can establish an almost iron-clad status cover. During all that time he would engage in no clandestine operations except to meet on rare occasions with his superiors from his clandestine organization, preferably when travelling outside his target country.

And then, when he is needed years later, he would be activated and placed in charge of a number of trusted agents, and would function as their clandestine operator. Such a clandestine operator is sometimes known as a "principal agent." Of course, there must be channels for such a principal agent to communicate with his headquarters and vice versa, which can be anything from dead drops, brush passes, or sophisticated techniques such as secret writing, microdots, radio, or other means of modern technology.

Regardless of the type of agent, be he a reporter in place, covert action agent, support agent, principal agent, or agent of influence, the clandestine organization must, of course, manage each one in accordance with the basic principle of cover, concealment, and compartmentation.

CHAPTER XI

The Files

While secret agents are the lifeblood of any clandestine organization, its files are its guts. The amount of information that quickly accumulates in those files in the form of reporting from abroad is astonishing, and can be invaluable to the organization and its customers.

A report of a relatively uninteresting conversation or else a description of a casual relationship between an intelligence operator and, say, a young army officer in a foreign country, or a diplomat, or the scion of a rich family, can be of immense value many years later when that person is, say, a top general, or a cabinet member, or a captain of industry, or if he is otherwise well-placed in an important organization. Diplomats, journalists, and military people, as well as clandestine operators, submit such reporting on a regular basis to their respective organizations.

We have made the reader familiar with Spotting Reports, Assessment Reports, and Activity Reports, but there is much more that can go into the files. Every clandestine activity must be reported and filed, so we have Casing Reports, Surveillance Reports and Counter-Surveillance Reports, Telephone Tap Reports, Clandestine Audio Reports, and so forth. Furthermore, there are Person Reports that summarize what is known about an individual, not to mention Information Reports covering political, economic, or military matters. In addition, most clandestine operations generate periodic Progress Reports summarizing such ongoing operations, and these too go into the files.

Retrievability

The critical aspect when accumulating and filing all these reports is <u>retrievability</u> of the factual matter they contain.

For example, the name of Myron Geflunction, a young diplomat from the Republic of Tilodia, might come up in reports from secret agents and clandestine operators. These reports might contain information on him, his activities, his associations, his character, and his personal foibles and tastes. His name might even come up in transcripts of telephone taps and bugging operations. Perhaps years later, Geflunction rises in his country's diplomatic service and becomes an important figure. The clandestine organization's customers might ask the organization for information about him. By then there might be voluminous material on Geflunction already accumulated in the files over the years.

An employee of the organization would then do a "name check" by searching for Geflunction's name in the organization's many documents that contain information on him. The employee would retrieve the documents, and then synthesize the voluminous information contained therein into one single information report.

Such a report could cover Geflunction's political and economic views, biographic material on his personal life, his personal and professional relationships, his tastes and peccadillos, his contacts, his career accomplishments, his supporters and his opponents, and so forth. The organization would then pass the summary report to its customers who would react with awe at the wide sweep of the clandestine organization's knowledge, which sometimes seems to border on omniscience in the eyes of those unfamiliar with how much information can accumulate over time.

It is imperative that the clandestine organization be able to retrieve all such information and combine it into a single report when requested to do so. In order to retrieve documents containing specific information, the person or the topic mentioned in each document has to have been already indexed. The index must cite each document itself and must record where the document is to be found in the clandestine organization's files. It's much like citing a topic in the index of a book and giving the page relating to it.

Pre-Computer System

The principles of a file system and the retrievability of its contents are the same for a sophisticated computerized system as for an old-fashioned hard-documents system. To better understand the basic structure of a system, we might consider a very simple, old-fashioned pre-computer system.

Perhaps the most rudimentary procedure is to assign a chronological number to each and every document that arrives at the clandestine organization's headquarters, then create a file card for each potentially retrievable item of information in each document, and note on the card the number assigned to the document and its date. (See Figure 11). Then one must file the document in numerical sequence in the organization's chronological document file, and file the card separately in alphabetical sequence in an index card file.

Later, when Myron Geflunction becomes an important figure in his country and rises to a high enough level to interest the clandestine organization's customers, one can go to the index, note all the file cards that cite Myron Geflunction, and make a list of the serial number of all the documents that contain information about him. Then one can retrieve the documents, and summarize them in a single report. Such a summary would also go into the files and would itself be carded. It would allow the summary to be retrieved if anyone wants to do a later check on him, and precludes the need to once again access each document that contributed to it.

The actual indexing will always be time-consuming. It can be brain-numbing work, during which employees of a clandestine organization spend hours and hours every day scanning incoming documents, indexing their substantive portions, and then moving on to the next document. But the job of reading incoming documents and indexing them is excellent training for future clandestine operators because it exposes them, on paper at least, to all kinds of operational activity described in many of the documents they scrutinize. It is also excellent training for those who later do the name checks, who retrieve the material, and who then collate and synthesize it into single reports.

TYPICAL INDEX CARDS

Gastresto, Smolip
Lt. Colonel, Degeneran Air Force
Named head of disbursement of secret intelligence funds
Chron Messg Degenera # 346, 3/8/2008

Hembersol, Samilio
Captain, Degeneran Air Force
Preparing for attache assignment
Chron Messg Degenera # 346, 3/8/2008

Miroflot, Refstar
Major, Degeneran Air Force
Will be trained as an intelligence operative
Chron Messg Degenera # 346, 3/8/2008

Ramstara, Frutis
Captain, Degeneran Air Force
Discharged for embezzlement
Chron Messg Degenera # 346, 3/8/2008

Air Force, Degenera
Subject File # 387519
Degenera Branch, Hqs.

People's Democratic Party, Degenera
Subject File # 389384
Degenera Branch, Hqs.

Pareto, Rop
Elected President,
Degeneran Hod-Carriers Union
Chron Mssg Degenera # 867, 5/7/1997

Pareto, Rop
Born: 10/12/1963, Rigera, Degenera
Personality File # 585-32189
Central Archives, Hqs.

Figure 11

But it does help to set guidelines as to what individuals and topics require indexing; for not everything in a document needs to be indexed. The people doing such work must have enough of an education to be able to read documents quickly and make judgments as to what might or might not be relevant for later retrieval. Those who have received basic training in clandestine operations would have particular insight as to the information that might be operationally significant when they are asked to do a synopsis of a potential recruitment target or of someone of counterintelligence interest.

One should reiterate, however, that such a procedure that requires the retrieval of many documents, each of which contains different information on a given subject, can also be time-consuming and very cumbersome. There are several ways to streamline the procedure.

Making it Easier: Creating Subject Files and Personality Files

Although a copy of each incoming document should receive a number for sequential filing in a chronological file, the retrievability of the information contained in them need not be from such sequential files. Instead, recourse to files becomes vastly easier if, in addition to a serialized chronological file, the organization creates a specialized subject or person file that contains copies of all documents in the chronological files pertaining to the given subject or person.

In that way, someone doing research on a subject or on a person could vastly simplify his search by retrieving the subject file or person file. He would, of course have to go to the office where the specific subject or person file is located in the organization, but that location would be recorded on an index card pertaining to the subject or person being researched. The procedure would be a lot less cumbersome than retrieving the myriads of separate documents in the organization's chronological file. (Figure 12 illustrates a typical filing system.)

The name-checker himself is the one who might create specific files on subjects or persons. For example, after doing a name check on Myron Geflunction, reading the chronological documents pertaining to him, and writing a full report on him, the person who writes the report can then create a specific personality file on Geflunction which would contain the checker's full summary report, and copies of subsequent documents referring to Geflunction. It would require only a single index card citing the file and noting the file's location within the clandestine organization, which would probably be the office that follows the organization's operational activity in the Republic of Tilodia, or else the file might rest in the organization's archives. Wherever the file is located, the main index card will state the place. Then the other cards can be destroyed and replaced with the single card that points to the file where <u>all</u> the documents are listed and summarized. Such a file might be the "Myron Geflunction Personality File," or perhaps a topic file "Foreign Diplomats in Raspasia." When additional information later accumulates regarding Geflunction, it too can be placed in a principal file, thereby precluding the need to search for it throughout various files in the organization.

As one can surmise, information on a given personality might also be found in other files not pertaining directly to that person but to other topics such as the Haephestian Army, the Mordinia Railway System, the Doofinia Civilian Intelligence Service, the Molusian Orthodox Church, the Finagle Ministry of Finance, the Degeneran People's Democratic Party, and so forth. If a previous summary has generated a specific personality file on the individual, then copies of the subsequent reports regarding him are eventually placed in such a file. Any subsequent reports that are summarized later, and the summary itself, can be placed in the same file.

Indexing and Filing - Conclusion

In sum, anyone doing a name check might uncover a number of cards leading to reports that contain references to the individual and perhaps also lead to a file on him. The name checker would then have to locate each document and each file, read them over carefully, and then write a coherent summary of the data relevant to the person that might be of interest to the clandestine operator abroad who requested the name check. As mentioned before, the name checker must be literate enough to do the job, and versed enough in the needs of clandestine operators to perform the name checks meaningfully.

The files of a clandestine organization are indeed its guts, and retrievability of information is essential if the accumulated material is to have any value. The work of reading, indexing, and filing documents, and later retrieving and summarizing them can be mind-numbing even with computerization, but it is of key importance and, as mentioned, requires highly-skilled personnel.

One simply cannot emphasize too much the importance of files in the activities and reporting of any clandestine organization. It is imperative that every clandestine operator understand the principles of information storage and of retrieval capability. Of course, computerization has vastly increased an organization's ability to store and retrieve the data it collects, but that is beyond the scope of this book. Nevertheless, the basic principles still apply.

RUDIMENTARY
FILING AND RETRIEVAL SYSTEM

INDEX
CARDS:

DOCUMENT:

BASIC
FILE:

Leads to file

Cites Subject,
Doc #, Date,
and Files Where
Doc is Located

Recorded
on card

Contains Material on
Subjects and/or Persons

Copies
for files

Chronological
File

Leads to file

Cites Person,
Doc #, Date,
and Files Where
Doc is Located

Recorded on card

Leads to file

OTHER
FILES:

Subject
File
(if any)

Copy for
chronological
file

Cites Subject File
(if any)
and File Location

Leads to file

Leads to file

Person
File
(if any)

Cites Person File
(if any)
and File Location

Leads to file

Copy for chronological file

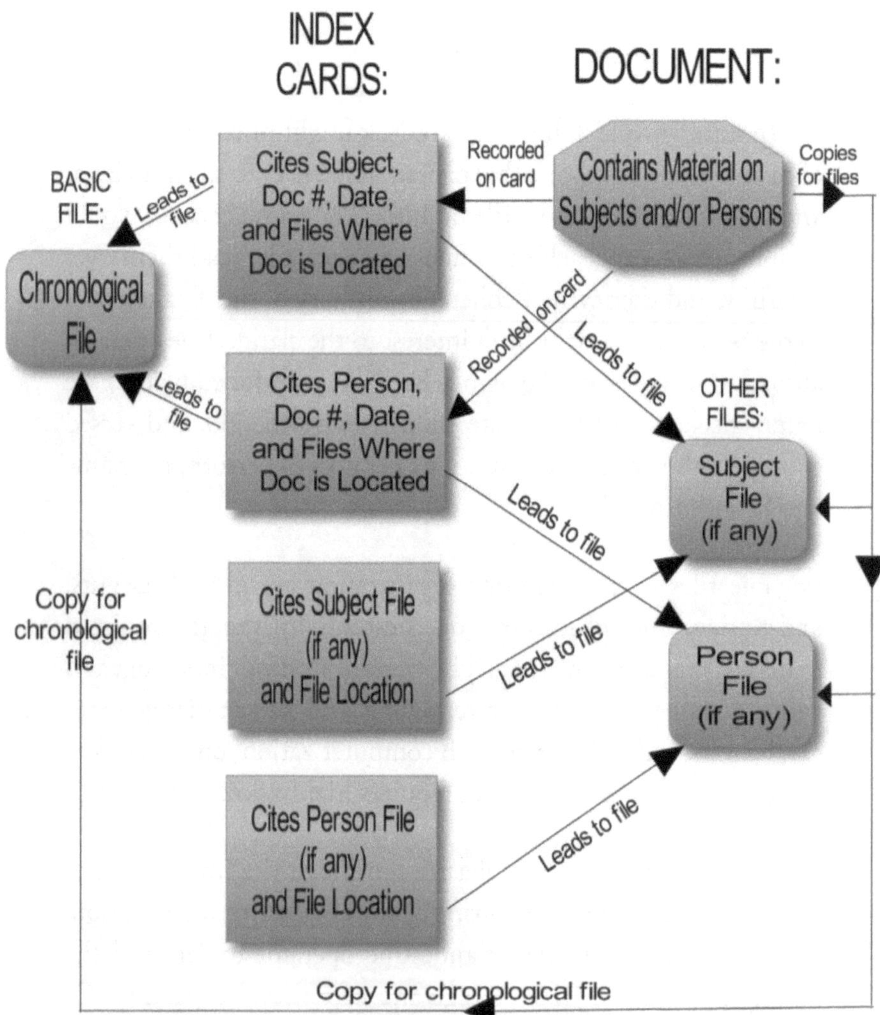

Figure 12

CHAPTER XII

Contemporary Considerations

The Burgeoning Complexity of Human Source Espionage

For centuries clandestine organizations could, with a modicum of efficiency, manage a group of secret agents in a target-country directly from the organization's headquarters. Such organizations could employ various means of communication with their operators who traveled back and forth to their home countries, or else communicated with their bosses back home by such means as coded messages or secret writing, and later with more sophisticated techniques such as microdots and radio transmissions.

But it soon became clear that political, economic, and military situations were becoming so fast-moving and the information about them so voluminous, that it was too difficult for a clandestine organization to collect information about them through separate clandestine operators or agents managed directly from home. Also, growing sophistication on the part of opposing counterintelligence services required a more complex and varying application of the principles and paraphernalia that underpin clandestine operations as elucidated in this book. The coordination of recruitment operations and of agent-handling activities, the administration of technical support, and the need to make quick on-the-spot decisions, required on-the-spot management.

What was obviously needed were local clandestine command structures that could accommodate not only clandestine operators, but also keep some records, provide a quick operational support capability, allow quick local decision-making, and also communicate with the organization's headquarters back home.

The Advantages and Disadvantages of Local Clandestine Command Structures

Although such command structures abroad would still be under the authority of the organization's headquarters, they would be headed locally by experienced clandestine managers with firsthand and direct knowledge of the local situation who could direct and coordinate local operations and react quickly to local events.

In the latter context, we should remember that the protective elements of cover, concealment, and compartmentation will never be perfect. There will always be the need to weaken some element of a clandestine operation to enhance another, so one must constantly tweak an operation to seek a proper balance between security and efficiency. Such a necessity becomes very problematic when the opposition becomes more and more adept, and when operations become more complex. The best judge as to how to tweak the imperfections in an operation in order to meet local challenges would be some experienced overall authority who is physically on the spot.

On the flip side, such command structures obviously put a strain on the applications of cover, concealment, and compartmentation. There is always the possibility of a gross violation of compartmentation if we centralize all clandestine operations within a foreign country. It presents the danger of a total compromise if the command structure itself were compromised.

Of course, if one of the clandestine operator-managers became known to the local professional opposition, perhaps as a result of an agent compromise, the opposition could put him under intense scrutiny and eventually compromise a number of other operations as well. But clandestine organizations hoped that well-crafted status cover for the operator-managers, plus their superior training and experience, would lessen the possibility of hostile scrutiny and afford a better chance of detecting it if it were to exist.

Liaison Relationships

Another factor that has affected most modern clandestine organizations is the development of formal relationships among friendly intelligence services. In an era of formal security alliances among nations, it is only natural and commonsensical that their respective security apparatuses - including their clandestine organizations - should exchange information and even work together to run some operations jointly.

Day-to-day communication and joint activity between clandestine organizations are obviously best carried out when each organization establishes a recognized presence in the other's country to communicate more readily with the host country's organization. But even though each organization is therefore aware of such a foreign presence in its respective country, such a presence is still under cover against the public opposition because usually neither side wants to draw public attention that an intelligence exchange is going on, or wants to reveal the identities of the individuals carrying it out. This is particularly true in cases in which an exchange is not always between totally amicable countries, and neither side wants the public to be aware of it. Even inimical countries often have a commonality of interests for which liaison intelligence sharing might be profitable.

Furthermore, even if the identities of clandestine operators are revealed in liaison relationships, they still must be protected to some degree from public scrutiny against the day that they are assigned elsewhere to operate under cover. Still, any clandestine operator who is directly engaged overseas in liaison work is obviously "known" to another service, so the knowledge of his identity becomes known to more people and will inevitably spread, which is why most clandestine organizations prefer to use older operators for liaison work in order to preserve the cover of younger personnel as long as possible.

Intelligence and security relationships can also yield perceptions as to the mentality and attitudes of the host-government regime. Such insights can usefully complement the reporting of our professional diplomats as well as conclusions from publicly available information. The foregoing is especially true in underdeveloped authoritarian countries. In such places, the dictator or the tribe or the faction that holds power often reserves the key military and security jobs for the fellow tribesmen, clansmen, or relatives whom they trust. Contacts with their security services can be particularly insightful; sometimes more useful than diplomatic contact. Indeed, even when countries have a tense or unfriendly attitude toward each other, it is often useful to have government-to-government relations in areas of mutual interest. Such interchange can be particularly valuable to maintaining contact that might prevent a more serious decline in relations.

EPILOGUE

Having come to this point, the careful reader should by now have grasped much of the thought processes and practices of professional clandestine operators.

Spycraft is more than operational security in which we apply cover, concealment, and compartmentation to counter different kinds of threats to various aspects of our clandestine activity. Of course, operational security is indeed a key ingredient in the thinking of a professional clandestine operator, but spycraft encompasses a lot more.

It is about psychological manipulation of people in order to acquire and then manage them as secret agents. It is about the creation of secure communication between clandestine operators and their agents. It is about the continuous application of counterintelligence techniques to validate and monitor secret agents. And it is about keeping files and records.

It is about reporting all clandestine activity involved in the spotting, assessing, developing, and recruiting of agents, about contacts with them, and about ancillary reports on physical locations and the movements of people.

Above all, it is about reporting information of interest to a clandestine organization's customers and about an intellectual grasp of the customers' information requirements. It is about coldly separating fact from inference, and about avoiding speculation and bias. Without good information reporting, much of a clandestine organization's efforts are for naught.

There is much misunderstanding among the public and among the customers of a clandestine organization as to the practice of spycraft. Many government agencies in many countries instinctively assume that clandestine reporting organizations merely elicit material from knowledgeable people, much as diplomats or journalists do. But in reality, spycraft is about acquiring and managing well placed <u>controlled</u> sources, and that is an entirely different thing.

I hope this book has shed some light as to what it's really about.